"*Amy offers the reader clear and concise guidance that has the potential to move the diversity conversation from simply a corporate concept to a transformative way of being.*" – **Tina Alexis Allen, Author of** *Hiding Out* **and Actor on** *Outsiders*

"*I have the privilege of knowing Amy both professionally and personally and know firsthand that she walks the walk, not just talks the talk in being an inclusive, culturally sensitive ally. Her book is not just academic theory, but is also based on lived experience. I believe it will make a great impact on the thought processes and hopefully the behavior of people who want to do the right thing in developing more diverse professional and personal networks, but don't know how or where to start.*" – **Sabrina W. Bristo, MSW, Human Services and Cultural Diversity Specialist**

"*In* Network Beyond Bias, *author Amy C. Waninger has written a book that sets the new standard for professional networking. As I completed my CHAMP matrix, I realized it's one thing to be aware of our biases, it is quite another to be intentional about overcoming them. Whether you a 'pro' at networking, or you are looking for ways to improve your networking, this book will blow you away!*" – **Jeff Ton, Technology Executive and** *Forbes* **Contributing Author**

"'Who is missing from my professional network?' It's a question I had never considered until reading Amy C. Waninger's groundbreaking and eye-opening book. But it's a question that gets to the heart of who I am — professionally and personally — and how my own biases might be standing in my way of helping others, growing my company, and even catapulting my own career beyond my current aspirations and (self-inflicted) limitations. Network Beyond Bias is a book whose time has come — a book that will improve teams, open doors, broaden careers, and bring a healthy dose of strategy, humanity, and perspective to the way readers think about the work they do, the hands they shake, and the success they achieve. Bravo to Amy C. Waninger for writing a book that's not just 'beyond bias' but also beyond our greatest expectations for how a book on diversity and inclusion can be as inspiring as it is practical." — **Kate Colbert, Founder & President, Silver Tree Communications and Silver Tree Publishing; Author of *Think Like a Marketer: How a Shift in Mindset Can Change Everything for Your Business***

"A pragmatic insight into unconscious bias and the power of networks. A must-read for any executive who genuinely wants to capitalise on the benefits of inclusivity." – **Gamiel Yafai, Author of *Demystifying Diversity***

"*Navigating your truth has never been more important and more challenging. In* Network Beyond Bias, *Amy C. Waninger shows you that there are spaces beyond personal prejudices that shine with shimmering solidarity, and she brings the diversity of these dimensions to new light with graceful determination and uncompromising devotion. The book is a pleasure to read and a must-have resource for business and academic professionals who are facilitating mindful communication with others in troubled times!*" **– José I. Rodríguez, Ph.D., Professor of Communication Studies, Long Beach State, and author of** *Interpersonal Communication for Contemporary Living*

"*With her new book* Networking Beyond Bias, *Amy C. Waninger offers a new perspective on expanding our networks that's useful and practical for the most junior employee right up the ladder to the executive suite. Her advice and examples are real and actionable, and will make you wonder how you didn't recognize your network blind spots before. Even those of us for whom diversity and inclusion is top of mind can benefit from Amy's approach which is generous and forgiving while still reinforcing the urgent need to diversify our viewpoints, connections and partnerships.*" **– Janet Whalen, Co-Active Career Coach for women at BeAmbitiousForHer.com, and host of the** *She Breaks The Mold* **podcast**

"I don't think we can ever talk enough about uncovering unconscious bias, effective networking, and working toward greater inclusion. In this book, Amy uses personal examples and simple language to continue the dialogue and get us into action. If you do nothing else, be sure to complete the networking exercise in Chapter 32. This unique approach will uncover gaps in your network that you never knew existed." – **Natalie Siston, Founder, Small Town Leadership**

"I would highly recommend Amy C. Waninger's book, Network Beyond Bias: Making Diversity a Competitive Advantage in Your Career. The book does a super job of integrating the importance of diversity and inclusion with the "who's and how's" of networking. The premise is by having a diverse group of connections it expands possibilities and offers more innovative ideas. Amy drives home the power of a diverse networkand offers suggestions to overcome perceived barriers when getting to know individuals who may be different from oneself. The book is an easy read and is filled with useful information including a tool to assess and measure the diversity of an individual's network. Real scenarios of diverse challenges provide the reader the opportunity to explore a variety of perspectives. The content included in the chapter, Seek Diverse Perspectives on Purpose, covers important facts about some of the most challenging and timely dimensions of diversity and inclusion. Because Amy shares some personal information and challenges she has experienced, after reading her book, I was left with the feeling of having a good sense of who she is and the value of what she brings to the field of diversity and inclusion." – **Jonamay Lambert, Founder and President, Jonamay Lambert & Associates, Diversity & Inclusion Expert**

Tim —
Who can you
include today?

NETWORK
BEYOND BIAS

MAKING DIVERSITY A COMPETITIVE
ADVANTAGE FOR YOUR CAREER

AMY C. WANINGER

Amy C Waninger

#CPCU 2018

Printed in the United States of America

First Printing, 2018

ISBN-13: 978-1-718681-51-4
ISBN-10: 1-718681-51-8
Library of Congress Control Number: 2018906105

Lead at Any Level, LLC
13009 Fairfax Ct
McCordsville, IN 46055
www.LeadAtAnyLevel.com

Ordering Information:
Quantity sales. Special discounts are available on quantity purchases by corporations, associations, and others who purchase directly from the publisher. Contact amy@leadatanylevel.com for details.

TABLE OF CONTENTS

FOREWORD

BY JENNIFER BROWN

I have had to reinvent myself many times in my career—from activist to opera singer, from opera singer to business owner and diversity expert.

Although such change is often accompanied by fear, I have come to not only anticipate each reinvention, but also to enjoy the process. I have learned to look around and ask, "Who can help me?" But also "Who can I help?" There is always someone else in my network who is also going through a similar process of transformation.

So much becomes available to us in times of change. It is an opportunity for us to do things differently, to challenge ourselves, to recalibrate to these times we live in. Sitting here and typing this in mid-2018, we are certainly living in times that require constant recalibration. We are far from powerless in shaping change, and have more tools than ever at our disposal.

But in order to be change shapers and makers, we must remain vigilantly self-aware and relentlessly open-minded. We must seek to become comfortable with being uncomfortable. After all, this is the crux of diversity. There is plenty to be uncomfortable about in the world, and plenty of ways in which we find our beliefs and our work challenged—now more than ever.

The question is, rather than pull away, can we lean into that discomfort? Can we seek difference in our workplaces, in our communities, and even in our friends? Can we grapple with the challenge we find ourselves faced with, and allow ourselves to be changed by it—both individually and collectively?

Amy writes that in our childhood, "We learn about values as if they were universal truths." As I have traveled my path, I have had to constantly re-evaluate and release many of the things I had been taught were universal truths. Instead, I had to learn to see myself in the context of those around me today. I am grateful for, and also reckon with, the privilege of my upbringing—such as my ethnicity and socio-economic background. Yet I, as an LGBTQ woman, along with many others who are underrepresented in business, continue to wrestle with an unequal world and the pain of stigma.

Straddling identities and life experiences, as all of us do, has been the greatest blessing in my life. I seek diversity around me. I seek to really "see" myself, to activate my role, and to ensure I am enabling the success of others. The network I have built around me allows me to practice this, every day. But this doesn't just "happen", for any of us—it needs to be created and fostered with intention, grace, and generosity.

There are great gifts to be discovered as we journey forward. As travelers, we are so fortunate to have Amy's "map", her wisdom, and her guidance as we traverse the winding path of change and grow into who we were always destined to be.

I am reminded of the African proverb: "If you want to go quickly, go alone. If you want to go far, go together."

Jennifer Brown

Speaker, Author, Founder, Humanist

NETWORK BEYOND BIAS

INTRODUCTION

Do you shy away from networking opportunities? Professional networking is critical for long-term career success. The more connected you are, the more opportunity you will create for yourself and others. But we don't readily recognize our default behaviors, nor are we aware of who is missing from our professional networks.

Is your professional network as diverse as the workforce and community around you? If not, you could be missing important opportunities for your career. We all face challenges in making meaningful connections, especially with people who differ from us in significant ways. Few of us consider the impacts of these missed connections. Even fewer know how to recognize and overcome them.

Do corporate conversations about diversity and inclusion leave you feeling...excluded? Regardless of your identity or job title, you may feel that corporate diversity training is a lot of fluff. When people in your industry talk about diversity and inclusion, you may think, "That's great, but what can *I* do about it?"

Do you want to build a reputation as a leader? Leaders can be anywhere, and should be everywhere – at all levels of an organization. Make no mistake: purposeful networking, building relationships on mutual trust, and considering multiple perspectives are all critical leadership skills.

> Visit the website for links to cited works and additional resources, organized by chapter.
>
> WWW.NETWORKBEYONDBIAS.COM

Network Beyond Bias: Making Diversity a Competitive Advantage for Your Career will help you assess and improve the breadth and depth of your professional network. You can remove the artificial barriers that may be keeping you from your next mentor, star hire, or big customer.

Are you ready to transform your career, one relationship at a time?

ABOUT THE AUTHOR

If you look at my resume or my LinkedIn profile, you will deduce that I am an experienced management professional with a background in Information Technology and the Insurance industry. On the surface, I may not seem a natural "diversity champion." One need not look too deeply, though, to understand why I am on this path.

My Diversity Story, Part 1 of Many

In high school, I frequently heard that my first-in-class math scores were impressive...for a girl. When I was a Computer Science major in college, total strangers told me I should go into Nursing or Education. Because those were good fields for women. When I worked as a programmer, my bosses praised my work; my peers told me I was very analytical...*for a girl*.

I later moved into analysis and design roles based on my exceptional ability to solve problems from an end user's point of view. I frequently heard that I had great people skills...for a programmer. When I first became a manager, some of my former peers said I was too young to lead them effectively.

As I developed my own leadership style, I vowed that I would never qualify my feedback or pigeonhole my team members based on their demographics, work histories, or untried skills. My approach has always been to help each of my team members identify their strengths and contribute in ways that excite them. Along the way, I have built teams that turned into "talent factories," mentored new managers, improved business processes, and bolstered the bottom line. I am convinced that this success was driven by valuing the diversity of my team members' strengths, interests, and backgrounds.

DIVERSE TALENT GETS DISCOURAGED

The diverse talent that *could* exist in many companies never gets in the front door.[1] If it does, corporate culture can be stifling. There is a lack of role models and mentors for members of underrepresented groups.[2] Promotions and rewards are often based on "cultural fit" over performance.[3] Managers don't know how to cross cultural boundaries to cultivate potential. Job postings list geographic requirements that candidates could easily overcome with technology and occasional travel. People fear having authentic conversations in the workplace.

I have worked primarily in two industries: technology and insurance. Both industries are struggling to find and retain talent.[4,5] Both industries lack diversity in their executive ranks.[6,7] I firmly believe the latter is the cause of the former. I want to do everything I can to turn these tides.

At first glance, I may not be an obvious diversity champion. Maybe you're not either.

And that's exactly why we need to be.

PART ONE: OUR BRAINS ARE BIASED

CHAPTER 1.
HOW YOU REALLY MAKE DECISIONS

Imagine you had to make an important career decision later today. You could be choosing your next mentor, approaching your next client, or hiring someone for a critical role on your team.

How much information would you need to feel confident in your ability to make a good decision? One hundred percent? Fifty? Twenty? Two?

How about just three ten-thousandths (0.0003) of one percent? That's one bit of information for every 275,000 available. What's more, that 1-in-275,000 plays to your specific fears and reinforces what you already believe to be true.

Perhaps you're very confident and believe you can make a good decision with such limited information. But would you trust the people around you – your boss, your customers, your coworkers, a hiring manager – to make that decision for *your* career based on 0.0003 percent of the available information? Probably not. But they are doing just that, and so are you, every moment of the day.

Before you close this book based on the 0.0003 percent of it you've read so far, please allow me to explain.

THE INFORMATION YOUR BRAIN IGNORES

Your brain can handle about 11 million pieces of information per second. However, your *conscious* thought capacity is only 40 pieces per second. [8] That means every second of every day, you are discarding 99.9997 percent of available information. Think about the decisions you make in those seconds – where to sit, what to eat, whether to start a conversation with a stranger, what to say when you do. You are making those decisions, every second of every day, with just 0.0003 percent of the available information.

Your brain considers what's relevant to you in the moment and discards everything else. You may be listening intently to your customer's concerns and not notice the buzz of the fluorescent lights in your office. Maybe there's movement at the far end of the room that takes your focus away from the customer. Perhaps your foot itches or you have a toothache. You could be preoccupied with any number of thoughts and completely miss what's going on right in front of you.

Your brain can't be everywhere at once. Instead, it tries to focus on what it perceives as important, interesting, or a potential threat. Every second of every day.

TAKE YOUR FOOT OFF THE GAS

What your brain does next is even more important to your decision making process. The feeling part of the brain, the amygdala, reacts to those 11 million sensory inputs before the thinking part of the brain has time to respond. You feel before you think.

---

amygdala, *noun*, an almond -shaped mass of gray matter in the front part of the temporal lobe of the cerebrum that is part of the limbic system and is involved in the processing and expression of emotions, especially anger and fear[9]

You may not know it, but unconscious bias affects you before your brain even knows what's happening! Don't believe me? Imagine you're driving late at night down a deserted highway. You look up into your rearview mirror and see a police cruiser with its lights flashing.

What do you notice about yourself first? Maybe your heart starts racing, you start to sweat, and feel nervous. You've probably already taken your foot off the gas.

Then, you start wondering why you're being pulled over. Depending on your age, race, gender, and driving history, any number of thoughts race through your mind. I even know one woman, Gina, who thought a police officer was pulling her over to commend her on her good driving!

Do you know what's happening here? Your brain starts making up a story to explain how you're feeling. You felt nervous first and then you try to find a reason for that feeling. (Except for Gina, of course.)

What happens when the police officer passes you and speeds on down the highway? Your mind says "WHEW!" but your heart takes a few moments to stop pounding.

This is a situation most of us can relate to on some level. It plays out in many aspects of our lives, in big and small ways, often without our even realizing it. This means that our feelings and gut reactions are in the driver's seat, unless we intervene.

Chapter 2.
Understanding Unconscious Bias

Where do these first impressions and gut reactions come from? They come from deeply-held preferences for or against certain things. That's what bias is: preference for one thing over another. My brain is biased, and so is yours. Bias means preference. It's nothing to be ashamed of. We are hard-wired for bias. Bias kept our species safe when we were primitive hunter-gatherers. We had to decide if each person we encountered was friend or foe. Knowing who was in our tribe and who wasn't was literally a split-second, life-or-death decision. Yet, despite all our cultural, social and intellectual adaptations, this biology still guides our thoughts and actions.

---

bias, *noun*, a particular tendency, trend, inclination, feeling, or opinion, especially one that is preconceived or unreasoned[10]

Bias starts very early in our lives. In our infancy, in fact. Studies show that infants as young as six months old demonstrate preference for people of their own race.[11] Even younger than that, babies show a preference for attractive faces over unattractive ones.[12] Newborns almost immediately begin to associate certain sounds and smells with comfort or pain. This, as you might have guessed, is only the beginning!

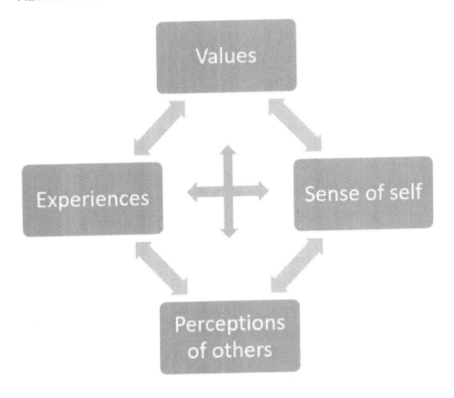

VALUES

During childhood and adolescence, we begin to adopt the values and norms of the culture around us. We learn about values (what is right and what is wrong) as if they were universal truths. Because they are as commonplace as the air we breathe, we typically do not think to question or challenge them.

values, *noun*, group conceptions of the relative desirability of things; deeply held convictions about what is important in life[13]

Our parents, teachers, and others expect us to conform to these values, praise us when we exemplify them, and punish us when we violate them. Our socialization is not complete, in fact, until we have internalized the expectations of our respective communities.

socialization, *noun*, a continuing process whereby an individual acquires a personal identity and learns the norms, values, behavior, and social skills appropriate to his or her social position[14]

SENSE OF SELF

As we develop physically, emotionally, and socially, we learn to shape our various characteristics into a sense of self, or social identity. This social identity is based on our experience in the world relative to other people: how strong we are, how we look, where we live, how we speak, how we dress or eat or worship or spend our free time. We form our sense of self based on those who are like us and those who are different. In part, we are basing our own identity on our perceptions of others.

social identity, *noun*, a person's sense of who they are based on their group membership(s)[15]

PERCEIVING OTHERS

As we firm up and fine-tune our sense of self, we also learn to make judgments – and I'm using that word on purpose – about others. Even as we define ourselves relative to others, we evaluate others from the perspective of our own identities. We gauge others' levels of success, virtue, worthiness not only against definitions we've created but also in relation to our own performance to that arbitrary standard.

> **We define ourselves relative to others,**
> **and we evaluate others**
> **relative to ourselves.**
> **#NetworkBeyondBias**

EXPERIENCES

But wait, there's more! We choose our experiences in ways that reinforce our identities and our perceptions of others. It becomes a vicious cycle. The less you vary your experiences, the more resolute you will be in your perceptions of others, and the more vested in your own identity.

Suppose, for example, that you see yourself as a "foodie," always willing to try new gourmet creations. When your friends call you to tell you about the new Vietnamese-German fusion restaurant in your neighborhood, you are likely to be among the first to try "pho schnitzel." But when those friends call you the following week offering tickets to *Professional Wrestlers on Ice*, you might decline. Both experiences may offer enjoyable time with your friends, but you are likely to choose the one that is consistent with your self-image.

Because our identities inform our choices and vice versa, we are constantly reinforcing, rather than challenging, our values and identities with the decisions we make and experiences we choose. Over time, our biases become so central to our identities that we no longer consider them. These *unconscious biases* then drive our decisions and behaviors in ways we don't readily recognize.

---

unconscious bias, *noun*, a preference that happens automatically, is outside of our control and is triggered by our brain making quick judgments and assessments of people and situations, influenced by our background, cultural environment and personal experiences[16]

We don't have to our limit ourselves in this way. ***We can choose to break out of this cycle***. We can instead choose to make more rational – and therefore, better – decisions. We can choose to open ourselves to new perspectives, more varied experiences, and conflicting ideas. We can choose to explore, or try on, different values and identities. In other words, we can choose to *grow*. These conscious choices, rather than our gut reactions, are what make us leaders instead of followers, heroes of our own stories instead of victims of circumstance.

Chapter 3.
Break the Cycle of Unconscious Bias

Having the power to break out of unconscious bias is one thing. Wielding this power won't be easy. You will have to recognize your own biases, confront your assumptions, and challenge your beliefs. You may even have to change how you see *yourself* in order to see others in a new way. It requires honesty, integrity, and vulnerability. Remember, this is the work of leaders.

> **You have to change how you see yourself**
> **so you can see others in a new way.**
> **This is the work of leaders.**
>
> **#NetworkBeyondBias**

Step 1: Put Yourself on Notice

First, notice your own responses to people, ideas, situations, and changes. Especially when you're in a new situation, you may feel anxious or excited or scared. When you notice that your heart starts racing or you feel a little uncomfortable, notice it.

You don't have to dive in to it in the moment. You don't have to judge, or critique, or feel guilty. But when you have time, ask yourself, "What caused me to feel that way?" Push yourself to think

23

about which identities, experiences, values, or perceptions may have led you to this type of response.

Then, you can evaluate whether those feelings are rational. The more you can back away from irrational responses, the more intentionally you can respond. Just noticing, as if you were observing yourself in the wild, can make a big difference in how you respond over time. In other words, noticing your biases takes away their power over you!

For example, I once noticed that face-to-face conversations with one of my team members, Deanne, made me uncomfortable. As I explored this further, I realized that I was fine when we were both seated, but not if we were standing. Why? Deanne is shorter than I am, and at 5 feet, 3 inches tall, I'm usually the shortest person in the room. Looking down to talk to her made me feel like I was being disrespectful, as if I were forcing her to "look up to me." When I understood what was driving my discomfort, I actually had to laugh at myself, and I was able to get over it pretty quickly.

STEP 2: OBSERVE THE RESPONSES OF OTHERS

Once you've begun to understand your own feelings and behaviors, you're ready to begin observing the responses of others. Again, I didn't say to judge. Think about what identities, experiences, values, or perceptions may have led someone to this type of response.

One thing I love about working with other people is that their responses – even to trivial changes – are so varied. Imagine your boss announced during a team meeting that liquid soap will be replaced with foam soap in the restroom. Chances are, somebody in the room will be excited about the new Foam Soap Initiative. On the other hand, there will invariably be someone else with their arms folded in opposition.

When you face a change or a new perspective, whether it's new soap dispensers or an industry paradigm shift, notice your own response first. Are you jumping in to help or scowling and crossing your arms? Then observe the responses of the people around you. You can file away all of these different responses like a database in your brain. The next time they replace the soap in the bathroom you can think, "Maybe crossing my arms isn't the only response to this. Maybe I could get excited about the change."

STEP 3: PRESS YOUR PAUSE BUTTON

> *"Between stimulus and response there is a space. In that space is our power to choose our response. In our response lies our growth and our freedom."*
> – Viktor Emil Frankl, M.D., Ph.D.

Finally, press your Pause Button. Once you have practice with noticing and observing, it's time to break out your next tool: The

Pause Button. This step allows you to think about other valid responses to situations, ideas, or people.

In his book *Everyday Bias,* Howard J. Ross advises us to PAUSE, which is his acronym for responding intentionally (116-117).[17] When you can consider multiple responses, you can choose the best one for the situation at hand. Better responses lead to better decisions.

When I hear the word "pause," I think of the pause button on a remote control. But where is the pause button on a person? As it happens, you have built-in pause button, called a *philtrum* or *medial cleft.* The philtrum is that little divot right under your nose. Most people aren't using their philtrum for much anyway. I say it's time to put this oft-neglected anatomical feature to work!

---

philtrum, *noun*, the vertical groove on the surface of the upper lip, below the septum of the nose[18]; also: *medial cleft, pause button*

Put your index finger on your newfound pause button. Do you look thoughtful and reflective? Good! You're well on your way! As an added bonus, pressing your pause button inhibits the flow of speech out of your mouth. This gives you time to take advantage of that precious space between stimulus and response.

When you're responding to a new situation, literally put your finger on your philtrum. Think for just a moment, and go through that mental database of all the possible responses you've observed. Only then, you can choose the best response for the situation. It won't be the same response every time; that's the whole point!

AN EXAMPLE

I started my career in Information Technology in 1999, when software developers were in high demand. The years that followed brought booms and busts. Companies would staff up for projects and then cut entire teams when various bubbles burst. The first time my position was eliminated, I was just a couple years out of school, had a limited professional network, and was six months pregnant with my first child. Panic is probably the best word to describe my reaction to the news that I would soon be unemployed. In the years and layoffs that followed, I found myself panicked each time my position was eliminated.

During one incident, though, I observed that the people around me were responding in different ways. Some had seen the layoff coming and were already interviewing elsewhere. A couple were investing their severance pay in new business ventures. Still others were having jovial conversations with IT recruiters in the area. *Sure, they're not panicked,* I thought to myself. *They have a lot of experience, and none of them is pregnant.* But then I came to a stunning realization. I wasn't pregnant anymore either! And I had more experience and a wider network than when I started my career.

By noticing my own reaction and observing the responses of others, I was able to change my own thinking. Within a couple of hours, I had a plan to learn as much as I could during the time I had left at the company. My new, purposeful response to the situation led to new opportunities and completely changed the course of my career. Over time, I became proactive at managing my career in the face of reorganizations, outsourcing and offshoring initiatives, and other forms of corporate upheaval. My next book, *Moving from Panic to Purpose: Responding to Changes in Your Career,* will help others do the same.

Sign up for updates about
my forthcoming book

*Moving from Panic to Purpose:
Responding to Changes in Your Career*

WWW.MOVINGFROMPANIC.COM

CHAPTER 4.
NEXT-LEVEL
BIAS-BUSTING

Recognizing your biases and exploring new responses can be exhausting at first. Once you get the hang of it, you may start looking for new ways to challenge yourself.

BREAK YOUR ROUTINES

In familiar situations, notice your routines. Do you sit at the same booth and order the same dish every time you go to your favorite restaurant? Do you talk to the same people each time you attend a networking event? When you drive to work, do you always take the same route? When you are a creature of habit, your brain's neuropathways become increasingly fixed, like water that carves a path down a hillside.

---

neuroplasticity, *noun*, the capacity of the nervous system to develop new neuronal connections[19]

For the next ten days, surprise yourself by doing something different or unexpected. Be spontaneous if you can; plan spontaneity if you have to. By changing your routines, you develop neuroplasticity.[20] You can literally create new paths for your brain. When you surprise yourself, you break out of "identity thinking." Instead of being "the kind of person who...," you can become someone with endless possibilities!

PUT YOURSELF IN A NEW SITUATION

Within the next 30 days, say "yes" to something you can't otherwise imagine doing. Attend a cultural event that is completely unfamiliar to you. Go to a cricket game or to the ballet. Attend a religious service outside your own faith. Take a pottery class or karate lesson. Pick anything you've never done before, and do it. Bonus points if you do it by yourself!

When you are in a new and unfamiliar situation, you will automatically spend more time observing the responses of others. You will have to rely on total strangers – and totally new perspectives – for social cues about how to dress, act, respond, and interact. When you don't have preconceived notions about your own responses, you'll be forced to adopt a different perspective quickly!

READ A BOOK

Reading a book may not sound like groundbreaking advice. After all, books have been around for centuries. Still, for very little cost and even less personal risk, books can help you learn about other views and cultures, develop empathy, and broaden your perspective. Here are some general ideas.

- A biography or autobiography about someone unknown to you
- History books or classic literature from another country or culture
- Any book by an investigative journalist that addresses both sides of a controversial issue
- Novels written for another audience, such as young adult fiction

As you read, consider why the main characters make the choices they do. Take note of passages that made you uncomfortable or that you found surprisingly relatable. Ask yourself how the book might be interpreted by someone whose background differs from your own.

Consider writing a review of the book to post on Amazon or your own blog. Finally, read the reviews others have written. Try to imagine how they may have come to a different understanding of the same text.

> Visit the website for book recommendations and printable worksheets to help you get the most out of this chapter.
>
> WWW.NetworkBeyondBias.com

Take an Implicit Association Test

Implicit association tests can help you discover the biases, stereotypes, and assumptions that guide your feelings and decisions.

These tests are available online for free, and the results are completely anonymous.

Visit https://implicit.harvard.edu/.[21]

> implicit association test, *noun*, a measure within social psychology designed to detect the strength of a person's automatic association between mental representations of objects (concepts) in memory[22]

(No, really, go take a test.)

Once you understand the nature and extent of your biases, you can imagine how they may be shaping your opinions, judgments, decisions. You may notice you've chosen to avoid certain relationships or experiences as a result of unconscious bias.

EXAMINE YOUR VALUES

Think about your values. How do you express them? How might others express these values differently? Look for these behaviors and then ask about the values that drive them. Consider how you might work with others to further your shared values, each taking a role that plays to individual strengths or forms of expression.

CHAPTER 5.
AFFINITY BIAS, IN-GROUPS, AND PRIVILEGE

Affinity bias is our tendency to surround ourselves by and spend time with people we believe are "like" us. When we do this collectively, we create *in-groups*. Almost everyone does this to some extent. We've all been in situations where we're hanging out with others who share our worldview. We may say or do things, without even thinking, that would make outsiders feel uncomfortable or unwelcome.

---

affinity bias, *noun*, the tendency to surround ourselves with people we believe are similar to us in some way

---

On the other hand, we've all been the new person at school or at work. We've all shown up somewhere under- or overdressed for the occasion. We've all felt like outsiders at some point. Sometimes our differences are obvious to everyone. Sometimes they're only – and often painfully – obvious to us. Whether we're "in" or "out" is usually circumstantial. When we find an environment where we're "in," we tend to spend more time there. It's more comfortable.

When our in-group is larger, has more authority to make and enforce rules, or determines the cultural norms of a larger group, we experience *privilege*. Privilege is a very charged word lately, so I'll give you a minute to collect yourself.

---

privilege, *noun*, (1) a right, immunity, or benefit enjoyed by a person beyond the advantages of most[23]; (2) anything you don't have to worry about on a regular basis that is a routine source of frustration or anxiety for someone else

---

THE NATURE OF PRIVILEGE

Privilege is not a constant state of being. Rather, it is relative and situational. When I go through a security line at the airport, I have the privilege of being white, cisgender, and able-bodied. But when I'm at the grocery store, I lack the privilege of being able to reach items on the top shelf due to my short stature. I have the privilege of not being seriously allergic to peanuts, so I don't have to worry as much about where my food is prepared. When I buy a new car, I lack male privilege, as I am statistically likely to pay more for the same vehicle[24] and anecdotally more likely to be cautioned about the "shiny gear shift" for the manual transmission (true story).

In any of these cases, having – or not having – privilege is not anyone's "fault." Privilege is not something you asked for or earned. However, being aware of your privilege (when you have it) will help you be more inclusive of those who don't share your good fortune. Furthermore, I believe that having privilege implies a certain *responsibility* to seek outsider perspectives.

Recognizing In-groups

Affinity bias leads us to create cliques, or in-groups, of people with whom we are similar in some way. These *in-groups* tend to be the social spaces where we're most comfortable.

---

in-group, *noun*, a group of people sharing similar interests and attitudes, producing feelings of solidarity, community, and exclusivity.

The trouble with in-groups is that they don't include everyone. So while you may feel perfectly comfortable at the office, someone else may feel like they're perpetually "crashing the party."

Assess Your Environments

Think about the places (real or virtual) where you interact with others in a professional setting. What do you notice about how people organize themselves socially? Are there rigid and defined groups, does everyone mingle freely, or something in-between?

Where there are groups, consider what those individuals have in common. Do they work in the same industry or have similar demographic profiles? When I started my career in IT, I tended to gravitate toward other people in the office who were around my age. In doing so, I missed out on opportunities to learn from people with more tenure. I also missed the opportunity to show potential mentors and sponsors that, despite my lack of experience, I had a lot to offer.

In many situations, I would also find that I was one of very few women in the room. Inevitably, I would form my strongest working relationship with another (possibly the *only other*) woman on my team or in my department. Without even realizing it, I was contributing to the gender divide. Instead of doing the hard work of exploring what I might have in common with people who were superficially different, I took the easy route. I can see now that it was a mistake. Who knows how many valuable connections I missed because of my tunnel vision!

I now seek people out based on more meaningful criteria. I want to know what they're working on, where they may have crossed paths with a mutual acquaintance, or whether they come from a different industry or culture. This is easy to do when you already work together, or if you're at an event where people are flowing in and out of conversations.

When cliques are already formed, making connections is much harder. Imagine yourself taking a deep breath and approaching the group that is the *least like you*. You're going to walk up and make that circle a diverse one just with your presence. "Hello," you say, as you shake hands all around. Now you can engage in some small talk and find someone with whom you share a common interest. For those of us who enjoy being in the in-group for most of the day every day, this may sound terrifying. But if you are in a minority group within your industry, this is an everyday occurrence.

CHAPTER 6.
A CAUTIONARY TALE

Often, we don't notice who's missing from our own conversations. What seems natural and inclusive to us may feel exclusive, or even hostile, to someone else. These conflicting points of view can have consequences we don't intend, for ourselves and for others. Keep in mind the following, fictitious example of HardNoggin Industries as you consider your own professional and social circles.

Our friends at HardNoggin Industries are trying to solve a serious problem. They have noticed lately that when things fall from the sky, it hurts their heads. Robin and Rita have come up with an ingenious idea. They want to institute a new policy requiring HardNoggin employees to wear hard hats, and they've already found a supplier!

When they share their idea, Diego and Dana agree this will make employees happier and save the company a lot of money. Everyone is excited and can't wait to try on their new HardNoggin Hard Hat.

WELL, ALMOST EVERYONE...

Fred is one of HardNoggin's newest employees. He's still learning about HardNoggin's business and getting a feel for the company culture. When he hears about the new policy, he has some concerns:

- Was he intentionally left out of the decision-making process?
- If so, was it because he is new to Hard-Noggin?
- Or does it have to do with his ... well, let's just say it... *whispers* Fred has a flat head. (No one at HardNoggin has mentioned it, of course, but it would be hard not to notice.)
- Is this new policy a way of telling Fred he's not welcome?
- Do they not know – or just not care – about the problems people with flat heads face in the Noggin industry?

What Should Fred Do?

- If he asks how the new policy affects him, he might be inviting trouble.
- If he follows the policy without question, he still has the problem of falling-object-induced head pain. He'll also have trouble keeping the hat on, and he'll feel silly.
- Maybe he could wear two hats, but that might be perceived as "flaunting" his flat head or as making fun of the new policy.
- Perhaps he's overreacting. Or maybe, just maybe, he should find a new place to work, where his flat head won't be an issue at all?

What Do You Think Happened at HardNoggin?

- Were Robin and Rita being malicious in their attempts to solve a problem?
- Did Diego and Dana set a policy designed to make Fred feel uncomfortable?
- How can Fred reconcile his specific concerns without calling attention to his "otherness"?

Let's assume that all the managers and employees at HardNoggin Industries are good people who care very much about each other. No one at HardNoggin wants to offend anyone, and everyone wants new employees to feel welcome. While this may not always be the case, it is *almost always* true that people have good intentions. It is also *almost always* true that people don't know what they don't know. Which brings us to...

WHAT HAPPENS IF WE DON'T CHANGE?

Let's think about some possible outcomes of the situation at HardNoggin, if not handled properly.

Work Environment

Left unchecked, the new policy at HardNoggin could create "us vs. them" factions. If Fred speaks up, the rest of team may get defensive and think Fred is overreacting. Suppose they talk about it amongst themselves, rather than with Fred directly. Excluding Fred from the discussion will make it more difficult to understand Fred's point of view.

If Fred doesn't speak up (after all, it's not his job to educate every round-headed person he encounters), he is likely to feel more and more isolated and resentful as time goes by. He becomes less likely to discuss the issues with the rest of the team and less likely to understand their motivations.

Outside of work, Fred probably spends time with other people who have flat heads. He'll tell them about his experience at HardNoggin and seek their advice. In any number of ways, Fred's experience could become folklore among his in-group. HardNoggin could be perceived as a bad place to work within the flat-head community. Over time, it will become more and more difficult for HardNoggin to hire and retain talented people with flat heads. The company might tell itself, "They're just not HardNoggin material," or "Fred is an exception. He's not like the other people with flat heads."

Groupthink

As HardNoggin continues to exclude "outsider" perspectives, the company will have difficulty developing products and services that have broad appeal. Assuming their competitors get this right, or as new competitors emerge, HardNoggin could lose market share.

> groupthink, *noun*, the lack of individual creativity, or a sense of personal responsibility, that is sometimes characteristic of group interaction[25]

Legal Challenges

Since the hard hat policy was implemented, Fred has been keenly aware of his "outsider" status at work. He applied for a position in product development and for a management role in Human Resources, but didn't get either promotion. In the lunchroom, he notices that he is often eating alone. Last week, someone invited Fred to a company picnic, telling him to "Be there, or be square!" Fred reached his breaking point. He's suing HardNoggin for discrimination and a hostile work environment. Now, HardNoggin management has both a legal problem and a public relations nightmare.

CONSIDER YOUR OWN "HEADEDNESS"

Think about a time when you felt like Fred, an outsider wondering if you were welcome in a group. What fears, concerns, or questions did you have? How did you resolve them? What was the outcome?

Now, identify a situation when you were part of the "in-group," having a "round-headed conversation" to the exclusion of someone else. Were you aware, at the time, that you were being exclusive? How did you experience this awareness at the time? How do you feel about it now?

What positive steps could you take to bridge the insider/outsider gap in your own working relationships?

> Visit the website for a printable worksheet
> to help you get the most out of this chapter.
>
> www.NetworkBeyondBias.com

NETWORK BEYOND BIAS

PART TWO: PUTTING THE WORK INTO NETWORKING

Chapter 7.
Effective Networking
Is A Super Power

The old question for success was "What do you know?" In the information age, though, we all have access to Google. Knowledge has become a commodity and is taken for granted. What you should be asking yourself instead is "What can you *do*, and *who* do you know?" In our global, social media-driven, freelancing economy, it has never been easier to get to know a wide variety of people.

---

network, *verb*, to cultivate professional relationships in a way that is mutually beneficial, creative, and expansive

---

What Networking Is...and Isn't

Networking, in many people's minds, involves some sort of smarmy, schmoozy, fast-talking fakery. Nothing could be farther from the truth! Real networking means understanding what people want or need, building trust broadly, and brokering relationships where everyone wins. For example, imagine you worked with Samir five years ago. He has since been promoted to management and is opening a new branch office in your hometown. You anticipate that Samir will need to hire a receptionist, a couple of sales agents, and an accountant. You introduce Samir to your childhood friend, Fatima, who just became a CPA. Now Samir is one step closer to reaching his goals, Fatima is on her way to full employment, and you are fondly regarded as the catalyst of their meeting.

MAKE YOURSELF VALUABLE, EVERYWHERE YOU GO

At one point in my career, I began describing my job as "Professional Networker." My job title was much less descriptive and had to do with managing data. But my *real* job was to connect people who had very specific questions about the inner workings of a business to people who had the detailed, if incomplete, answers that they had forgotten years ago. Sometimes I could make that happen with one phone call or email. Most of the time, though, it involved tracking down numerous false leads, analyzing org charts, sifting through documentation, and getting creative with my questions. A colleague once told me that his team referred to me as a superhero because I was able to help them so consistently.

It took me a while to recognize my role as a Professional Networker. But once I came to the realization that I had this ability, I started to see how I could apply it in other contexts. By expanding my network, I began to synthesize information across disciplines and industries. I was better poised to connect more people to each other and to new ideas. By getting out of my cubicle, I found new answers to "What can you do, and who do you know?" As a result, I've created new opportunities for myself and others.

And you can, too.

Even If You're New to the Workforce...

Even with no professional experience, you can make great things happen for people in your network. Listen to them and ask open-ended questions. Once you understand what kinds of problems people are working on or what they're interested in, send them occasional links to articles or blog posts on those topics.

...And Especially in the Gig Economy

Networking in the freelancing space, or gig economy, saves time and money. Morgan, your blogger friend, might need an infographic for some cornerstone content. Your coworker Shae has a side hustle as a graphic designer and will do a great job. Your recommendation can help Morgan sift through the noise of a million freelance options to find Shae's storefront. Their small transaction via Fiverr or 99Designs, for example, can lead to a long-term relationship and more lucrative contracts. When you connect gig workers, you are introducing people for low-risk interactions, because there is relatively little money involved. They will build trust with one another over time, meaning you need to lend very little credibility to the initial exchange.

CHAPTER 8.
ALLOW ME TO INTRODUCE YOURSELF

Knowing who you are and understanding your unique value is the foundation for successful networking. Are you your own worst critic, disproportionately attuned to your mistakes, shortcomings, and weaknesses? To network effectively, you must instead recognize all that you offer.

WHAT MAKES YOU YOU?

As you learned in Chapter 2, your self-image is formed throughout your whole life, in response to the world around you. Because it is so central to your understanding of the world, it may be difficult for you to articulate how you see yourself. Having a clear picture of your strengths, values, and work style will help you find the people and opportunities that are the best fit for you.

---

self-image, *noun*, the idea, conception, or mental image one has of oneself[26]

When you're networking, it's also important to understand how *others* see you. The collective perceptions of others is what forms your "personal brand." Knowing what sets you apart – what specific things you do better than others – will help others find you.

Use the tools and activities that follow to get a well-rounded picture of what makes you...YOU.

---
personal brand, *noun*, the idea, conception, or mental image that *others* have about you

---

PERSONAL ASSESSMENTS

Personal assessments are everywhere these days. They can be incredibly useful in helping you understand yourself and your brand. Here are some of my favorites.

StrengthsFinder 2.0 *and* Strengths Based Leadership

My personal favorite, Tom Rath's *Strengths-Finder 2.0* tells you what work energizes you and how to maximize your strengths.[27] *Strengths Based Leadership*, by Tom Rath and Barry Conchie, provides additional insights for managers and leaders about how they lead and engage their teams.[28] Each copy of *StrengthsFinder 2.0* and *Strengths Based Leadership* includes an access code for a free assessment. You can also skip the books and take the assessment for a small fee at www.GallupStrengthsCenter.com.[29]

Fascination Advantage

Marketing expert Sally Hogshead has adapted corporate brand analysis processes to help individuals understand their *personal* brands. Her website, HowToFascinate.com, offers a free personality test that reveals how the world sees you.[30] I took this assessment recently, and am still reading through the report. Hogshead's books, *How the World Sees You* and *Fascinate,* offer additional insights.[31,32]

DiSC Profile[33]

DiSC stands for Dominance, Influence, Steadiness, and Conscientiousness. Your DiSC profile tells you the extent to which you use each of the styles at work. Understanding your DiSC profile can help you improve communication and find a more balanced work style. From a networking perspective, this assessment can help you identify the connections you need to create balance in your network. What's more, it can help you adapt your communication style to attract those people!

Myers-Briggs Type Indicator[34]

The Myers-Briggs Type Indicator (MBTI) helps you understand your personality across four dimensions. For each dimension, you answer questions that indicate your tendency toward one of two polarities. The assessment results in one of sixteen personality types with initials like ISTJ or ENFP.

Pottermore Sorting Hat[35]

I included this one just for fun! This assessment is based on the *Harry Potter* novels by J.K. Rowling. Find out if you lead with courage, intellect, kindness, or whatever-is-good-about-Slytherin at

J.K. Rowling's pottermore.com. This assessment gets bonus points for being an excellent conversation starter at networking events.

> Visit the website for links to
> these resources and more.
>
> WWW.NETWORKBEYONDBIAS.COM

LOOK TO YOUR NETWORK

If you want to fully understand how *others* see you (your "personal brand"), you're going to have to do some digging. Here are four suggestions to help you on your mining expedition.

Talk to Your Coworkers

The people with whom you work the most closely are likely to have valuable insights about how you are perceived. Use questions like:

- Can you describe your experience in working with me?
- When my name comes up in the office, how do people respond?
- What's the "water cooler talk" about me / my performance / my potential?
- When have you seen me at my best?

Write down the words they use. Look for themes around your strengths. Schedule time to follow up with them on "trouble spots." (Do follow up later. But right now, we're focused on positives.)

Read Past Performance Reviews

If you've worked at the same company for many years, or if you are a hoarder, you likely have access to past performance reviews. These can be valuable in helping you spot year-over-year trends. Start as far back as you are able, and read them chronologically. Do you see a story unfolding about how you've developed new skills, resilience, or professional maturity? Have different managers given you similar feedback over time? What accomplishments make you most proud? Write down your thoughts, and return to it when you are ready to craft your elevator pitch.

Conduct a Personal Brand Survey

Free survey tools abound. You can easily create a survey on Google Forms, SurveyMonkey, or other sites. Set up a quick survey, and email a link and an explanation to people you trust. Or blast it out on LinkedIn for the whole world to see. You'll be amazed at how many people are willing to help you, if you only ask.

Not long ago, I sent a personal brand survey out to my network. My goal was to get as much feedback as possible about how others see me. It actually worked! The words my current and former colleagues used to describe me were consistent. Their "impact statements" gave me the courage to embrace what makes me, me. As odd as it may sound, the personal brand survey gave me permission to be the me-est I can be.

> The people in your network are giving
> you clues about your personal brand.
> Are you listening?
> #NetworkBeyondBias

Create a Compliment Journal

If you're not good at accepting compliments, it's time to develop this important skill. Learn to listen to the positive things your coworkers say to and about you. They are telling you what they admire about you and what they value. Keep a list of these interactions, and see what patterns emerge.

CHAPTER 9.
MAKING CONNECTIONS

The first time you attend a networking event, you may be as nervous and uncomfortable as I used to be. Take a deep breath, relax, and know that it does get easier with practice. Pretty soon you'll find yourself networking at the grocery store or your child's soccer game without realizing you're doing it!

STAND OUT

At any networking event, be a pop of color in a sea of gray suits. Smile. Consider wearing something distinctive as a conversation starter. (One of my Associates and self-proclaimed Insurance Nerd, Tony Cañas, wears a Superman t-shirt under his sport coat.) Ask good questions, look for a connection, and offer to help. So many people are only out for themselves. By putting out a different vibe, by expecting nothing for the value you offer, others will be drawn to your energy.

> Ask good questions, look for a connection, and offer to help. #NetworkBeyondBias

Have an "Elevator Pitch"

Using the material you gathered in Chapter 8, work up a 30-second introduction for yourself. Someone will inevitably ask, "So, what do you do?" You'll want to have a clear and concise answer to that question.

elevator pitch, *noun*, a succinct and persuasive sales pitch

The idea is not to recite the same 75-word script every time you meet someone new. On the contrary, you want to be confident, casual, and natural in the way you explain who you are and what you create in the world. Be consistent in your messaging without sounding rehearsed in your delivery.

Give Without Expecting a Reward

When you meet someone, introduce yourself with a smile, eye contact, and a warm handshake. Ask friendly questions and be an active listener. Look for common interests or experiences that might give you "in-group" status on some level: your kids may go to the same school, you share a love of opera, or you both cheer for same basketball team.

Ask what interested them about the meeting or what their connection is to the organization. Chat for a bit to see if you can help the person in some way. If they're complaining about yard work, perhaps you can recommend a reliable lawn care service. They may be looking for a new book, and you know of a great paperback (*ahem*) to recommend. Finding a way to help gives you a reason to ask for their contact information. You'll learn about staying connected in the next chapters.

Tips for Using Business Cards

In any social situation, there are unwritten rules of behavior, and opinions will vary. The exchange of business cards is no exception. In Asia, for example, there is a formal protocol for accepting someone's business card. In the United States, however, just about anything goes. Still, I find good manners go a long way in creating the all-important first impression.

Always ask for someone else's business card before offering your own. Be sure to tell them that you would like to contact them for a specific purpose, and be sure that purpose isn't to sell them something. Remember, you're building relationships for the long term, not offloading excess inventory. After they've handed you their business card, you may respond in kind. Conversely, if someone asks for your card, always ask for theirs in return.

"What if I don't have business cards?"

I'm a big fan of creating your own business cards for personal use. Don't use your employer's logo – or even the company's name. A simple white card with your contact information will suffice. You can print your own cards or order more professional ones. Sites like VistaPrint and Moo offer high-quality options at affordable prices.

Include your name and phone number at a minimum. Your email address should be simple and professional, ideally some variation of your first and last name. If you don't have an email address that matches your name or personal brand, set up a free account at Gmail or Outlook.com.

> **If your employer doesn't provide business cards, make some of your own.**
>
> **#NetworkBeyondBias**

Consider including a tag line that reinforces your personal brand. For example, you can list the Strengths, Fascination Advantage, or key word you discovered in Chapter 8. If you're looking for a job, you might list a couple of your most marketable skills.

Finally, if you use social media in a professional way, include these handles in your contact info. I recommend including your LinkedIn profile so you can build your virtual network as well. This will also come in handy for making introductions, which is the topic of Chapter 10.

Leave some "white space" on the card. That way, you can write down a referral or recommendation as you give it away. Or, the recipient can capture a brief note about where you met and what you discussed.

FOLLOW UP

When you get home, go through the business cards you collected. Send a LinkedIn connection request, along with a personal note, to each person you met. If appropriate, follow people on Twitter or other social media platforms. Follow through on any promises you made to provide information, contacts, or other resources. Then, you'll want to consider what introductions you should make within your network.

CHAPTER 10.
CONNECTING OTHERS

HOW TO MAKE INTRODUCTIONS

I prefer to make introductions via LinkedIn whenever possible. This allows each party to research the other before making any further commitment. It also allows either party to opt out without having their personal contact information exposed. To give you some ideas, I've included some examples of connections I've made in my own network.

Job Opportunity

You'll learn about the dark side of airplane conversations in Chapter 20. But in a more productive scenario, I made the acquaintance of a seatmate who happened to be hiring in a high-demand field. As luck would have it, one of my former colleagues was launching a job search for just such an opportunity!

> Daniel – I just met Vijay on a plane. He works for <company> as a management consultant for their growing data strategy practice. You should connect with him to learn about what he's building over there!
>
> Vijay – Daniel has executive-level expertise in data strategy. He is looking for new opportunities in the consulting space.
>
> Happy connecting, gentlemen!

Media Exposure

Immediately after meeting with podcast host Janet Whalen (whom I first met on Twitter), I set out to connect her with as many women as possible (and a few men) who might want to be interviewed on her show. In total, I connected her with more than a dozen entrepreneurs, authors, and community activists who could help her achieve the goals of her podcast. On the flip side of that equation, several people in my network are now getting a platform to spread their message and build their personal brands.

> Janet – Mary is a lawyer, cybersecurity expert, and former FBI agent. She mentors dozens of young women and leads an organization that seeks to diversify the cybersecurity industry.

> Mary – Janet hosts *She Breaks the Mold* podcast, which features women whose work lifts up other women. I'll be interviewed for her show in June, and I'm connecting her to amazing women I know who meet her show's criteria.

I was delighted to hear Mary's story on *She Breaks the Mold,* just a few weeks later.

Business Partnership

In another case, I had met two women at different conferences (on opposite coasts!) who were both entrepreneurs in the research consulting space. I suspected they might have occasion to rely on each other's expertise and asked each of them for permission to make the connection.

> Ladies! Since you are both in the research consulting field, I thought you might benefit from connecting. If memory serves correctly, Amanda works in qualitative research, and Margaret in quantitative. I don't know much about research consulting, but it sounds like a potential collaboration opportunity. Happy networking!

Request for Information

Jena announced on Twitter that she was moving out-of-state and needed some help with the transition. I asked Jena to send me a LinkedIn invitation so I could help. She is now connected with Gina, the leader of a California resource center for HR professionals, whom I had met when speaking at a conference just a few weeks prior.

> Gina, Jena is an HR professional moving to California. She has questions about state-specific regulations. I am hoping you can be a resource for her. Happy connecting!

BEST PRACTICES FOR INTRODUCTIONS

The most important aspect of making introductions is to be intentional about matchmaking. I wouldn't have connected research consultant Margaret to management consultant Vijay. Similarly, I wouldn't have sent HR professional Jena to just anyone on the West Coast; I connected her to someone who runs an association specific to her needs.

When making introductions, be clear about what each person needs and can offer the other. Explicitly state the reason for the match, and be transparent about the extent of your existing relationships. Use genuine praise when warranted, and never vouch for someone beyond your personal experience with them. Saying a total stranger is "the best marketing consultant in the business" dilutes your credibility. For example, I stated that my knowledge of management consultant Vijay's background was limited to what he told me on the plane. On the other hand, referring to long-time colleague Daniel as "an executive-level expert," conveys the level of trust I have in making that recommendation.

Another critical factor in making introductions is to ask for nothing in return. No finders' fees, no requests that they "return the favor" or "owe me one." Any genuine effort to help others builds trust, creates value, and elevates your standing among your colleagues. To that end, I hope my friends will forgive me for using real examples for the sake of authenticity and credibility.

WHEN A RECRUITER CALLS

Many people I know tell me they hang up on recruiters. Excuse me?!? Recruiters are *fantastic* people to have in your network! You're likely to be looking for a job someday, or know someone who will be.

You may or may not be looking for a new position. The recruiter won't know until he or she asks. The job the recruiter is seeking to fill may or may not be your dream job. You won't know until you ask!

> **When a recruiter calls, answer the phone!**
> **#NetworkBeyondBias**

Even if the position isn't a good fit for you, ask some questions about the open role. What level of experience is required? Which skills are most important? How large is the company, and what industry does it serve?

Ask the recruiter for an email address or phone number to send referrals. Forward that contact information out to a few people in your network who might be a good fit for the role. Or consider sharing the open position on social media. You may be the link between a casual connection and their next opportunity. Imagine how much that could do for your relationship!

PART THREE: FIVE CRITICAL CONNECTIONS

"We are the average of the five people we spend the most time with."
– Jim Rohn

CHAPTER 11.
WHERE TO BEGIN:
YOUR CHAMP NETWORK

Professional networking is essential for the longevity of your career and your company. Yet, many people cringe when the subject of networking comes up. If you are new to networking, you may have no idea where to begin. My advice is to start building strong relationships with the people closest to you, and start now. In this section, you'll learn the five critical connections for your career: your CHAMP network.

> **Start building relationships with the people closest to you, and start now.**
>
> **#NetworkBeyondBias**

CHAMP NETWORK, IN SUMMARY

CHAMP is an acronym that stands for **C**ustomer, **H**ire, **A**ssociate, **M**entor, **P**rotégé. Your CHAMP network is important because it's the people *you choose* to have in your professional life. If it is true that you are the average of the five people closest to you,[36] then you must be intentional when filling your CHAMP network.

By seeking Customers, Hires, Associates, Mentors, and Protégés for your network, you will gain a broad and deep perspective of your industry, your company, your skills, and your career. Your Customers will give you a fresh perspective on your industry and company. Having a strong Hire Network will allow you to help others, create opportunities, and solve problems. Work with Associates to fill in the missing pieces of your big picture (and theirs). Mentors will show you the way forward, and Protégés will remind you how far you've already come. Finally, when you make connections to help others build their CHAMP networks, your value increases many times over.

CHAPTER 12.
CUSTOMER NETWORK: YOUR KEY TO FIRST-HAND MARKET INSIGHTS

Regardless of your industry, company / organization, or your specific role, you need to understand your customers. Customers will know things about your company and your industry that you do not. The best way to understand your customer is to build a strong, professional relationship with one of them. First, let's define who counts as a Customer, and who does not.

WHAT IS A CUSTOMER?

For our purposes, "Customers" include both actual customer and *potential* customers for your business or industry. Customers have a choice and may (or may not) choose to pay you or your company for the goods and services offered in an open market. If you work for a college, your Customer is any adult who wants to learn. For a bank, your Customer is anyone in your community who has or needs money. If you work for an insurance agent, your Customer is anyone who owns a home, automobile, or business.

Your Customers' Customers may also be your Customers. For example, if you work for a newspaper, you may sell ad space to a local bakery. The bakery is your Customer for the ad space you sell. In turn, the bakery is hoping to reach its Customers through your newspaper. The bakery's Customers are hungry people in the metropolitan area. Should your newspaper lose sight of the needs of hungry people in the metropolitan area, you may also lose the ad revenue from the local bakery.

---

customer, *noun*, one that purchases a commodity or service[37] (or one that has that potential to do so)

Anyone who *could be* buying your product or service is a Customer. If they *are* buying from you, learn about their experience working with you or your company. If they are buying from a competitor, find out why. How is your competitor differentiating its products or services? What can you learn from your Customer Network about trends in the market, the competitive landscape, and the quality of your products and services?

WHAT ABOUT INTERNAL CUSTOMERS?

For our purposes, people inside your company are *not* Customers. They are your business partners, working in collaboration with you, on behalf of the company, for the benefit of its stakeholders. There seems to be a push in business to talk about "internal customers." While there may be some merit in that discussion, I have found that it allows us to take our collective eye off the ball. Even if someone working for your company purchases the company's goods and services, don't count them as a part of your Customer Network. They have access to the same insider lingo you do. Their blind spots and biases are likely similar to yours. They do not have the unique "outsider" perspective that you need to see your industry or your company from a fresh point of view.

CHAPTER 13.
HIRE NETWORK:
SURROUND YOURSELF WITH
TALENTED PEOPLE

Almost everyone, at some point in their career, needs a little help finding a job. The better poised you are to help them find a good fit, the more goodwill you will create in your network. I am not recommending that you hire your friends to fill your team. Rather, when you meet other professionals, consider whether you to include them in the pool of people that you connect to hiring managers and other job leads, your Hire Network.

IF YOU ARE NOT A MANAGER (YET)

Even if you're not a manager (yet), you need a Hire Network. Someone in your network is probably hiring right now. Someone else you know may be a perfect fit for that open role. Are you positioned to make that connection? If so, provide a "warm transfer" referral by introducing the two individuals to each other. Referrals are as good as – and possibly better than – hires. (No one wants to network like a CRAMP, so the word that started with *H* won the spot in the acronym.)

Many people who are managers today did not set out to become managers. Yet sometimes an opportunity or promotion is just too good to pass up. Those that come into management with a strong Hire Network are well ahead of the game!

IF YOU ARE ALREADY A MANAGER

If you manage a team of people, you will inevitably find yourself needing to hire someone. Rather than hope for the best when the open position goes live, you should be working *now* (read: always) to build a pipeline of people who could join your team. Talk to the people in your industry, as often as possible, about their strengths, recent successes, and career ambitions. When a spot opens on your team, make sure you get the word out in your Hire Network. You'll be able to fill jobs more quickly and with more qualified people.

As a manager, you likely work with other managers quite a bit. When others are hiring, find out what skills, capabilities, and qualities they are seeking. Making connections to talented people in your Hire Network will help everyone involved.

Visit the website to download
"Simple Steps to Reduce Bias in Hiring"
WWW.NetworkBeyondBias.COM

CHAPTER 14.
ASSOCIATE NETWORK:
YOUR EYES AND EARS ACROSS THE INDUSTRY

No matter where you work or what you do, you need a strong Associate Network in your company, industry, and beyond.

Associate Networks are made up of your peers, or people with a similar level of authority as yours. Whatever role you play in an organization or industry, you are likely in good company. New employees, first-time managers, and seasoned executives can all have strong Associate Networks. Anyone you work with on a regular basis is likely in this network. Because you work closely with them, you should be able to build relationships naturally.

---

associate, *noun*, peer

Imagine your industry – or your company, if it is large enough – as a giant jigsaw puzzle. Your role or department is represented by one oddly-shaped piece. By networking with peers in other departments of your company or other companies within your industry, you get to see more pieces of the puzzle. When you can put enough of them together, you get a big-picture view, no matter how small your part may seem.

BE A MEERKAT

Meerkats work as a team to find food and look out for threats. A meerkat digs around for a while, but then it pops up to make sure all its meerkat buddies are still around, doing meerkat things. If you never pop up to see what your buddies are doing, you might find yourself all alone on the prairie.

ASSOCIATE NETWORKS ARE THE EASIEST OF ALL

Of all the CHAMP networks, Associates are the easiest to find and engage. They are all around you, and you see them every day.

Because there are fewer power dynamics involved, peer connections are usually less intimidating. You already have a lot in common, and you probably have a lot to learn from one another.

WHERE TO BEGIN

Start by inviting an Associate out for lunch or a cup of coffee. Get beyond superficial small talk by asking friendly, open-ended questions.

- How did you get to your current role?
- What excites you about the work you're doing right now?
- What challenges are you facing right now?
- What's next for you?

You will be amazed at what you can learn about other departments, other companies, and other people over a simple cup of coffee! The more people you can engage in these conversations, the more you can learn.

When your turn comes around to share, keep the conversation honest and positive. Don't be afraid to share challenges you've overcome, your short-term goals, or your long-term aspirations. Avoid placing blame for problems, and never speak ill of a colleague or manager. Remember, you may be a candidate for your Associate's Hire Network someday!

Chapter 15.
Mentor Network:
A Glimpse into the Future

Mentors are people who have more experience, or different experience, in your field. A Mentor can help you with a short-term or long-range goal. He or she can help you imagine possible futures for yourself or likely outcomes of decisions you're facing. A Mentor can also help you build your network over time by introducing you within their professional circles.

---

mentor, *noun*, a trusted counselor or guide[38]

Is there someone in your company or industry you admire? Tell them so! Ask if they have 30 minutes once a month (for example) to help you grow in your career. Be genuine and proactive, and be gracious even if they say no.

 Is there someone in your company or industry whom you admire? Tell them so!

#NetworkBeyondBias

Engaging with a Mentor can be time well spent. To build a successful relationship, be proactive. Have goals for the mentorship and communicate them clearly. Know which aspects of your career or development require the Mentor's guidance, and come to each conversation prepared with an objective or desired outcome. Be respectful of and grateful for your Mentor's time by demonstrating that you are following their advice.

You may find that you admire the strengths or expertise of different people. That's wonderful! Try to establish a Mentor Network that is as well-rounded as you wish yourself to be.

Chapter 16.
Protégé Network:
A Reminder of How Far
You've Come

Last, and perhaps most important, is your Protégé network. A Protégé is someone you mentor, plain and simple. The word connotes some sort of Jedi/Apprentice relationship, I know. You probably *are* a Jedi Master in some aspect of your work. Develop a plan to share that knowledge with someone just coming up in your field.

> protégé, *noun*, one who is protected or trained or whose career is furthered by a person of experience, prominence, or influence

Why Is This Important?

There is always someone, somewhere who needs to see a possible future version of themselves. For every person who has made it through school, out of poverty, beyond an illness or addiction, to the other side of bad choices, or into a profession, there are dozens of people who can't see a path forward. For every one of us who has gotten a promotion, there are dozens of people just entering the workforce with no idea how to proceed. Did you have a mentor or role model? If so, what did that mean for you? If not, how might you have accelerated on your path if someone had shown you the way?

The more you know, the more you realize you *don't* know, and the less you realize you *do* know. Wow. That's a paradox, isn't it? This tendency of our confidence to be inversely related to our competence is called the *Dunning-Kruger Effect.*[39]

Imposter syndrome[40], the fear that everyone will find out you're a big ol' phony, increases with our level of achievement and mastery of a subject. We often devalue the skills we've mastered *because they're easy for us.* News flash: Everyone didn't learn what you did the moment you learned it. Spending time with someone who hasn't learned it yet can be a great reminder of how far you've come. Doing so also gives you an opportunity to share your knowledge for someone else's benefit. Everyone wins.

---

imposter syndrome, *noun,* as a collection of feelings of inadequacy that persist despite evident success[41]

The more you give, the more you gain. I don't have any science to back this up. Anecdotally, this is real, and I see it in my life every single day. Sure, there are wildly successful jerks. Just don't be one of them.

Putting good out into the world also improves your self-esteem. When you "pay it forward," other people are drawn to you. All those people you helped will celebrate with you when you make it big. As Dick Parsons said in his 2016 interview with *Fortune* magazine, "Be the person everyone wants to see succeed."[42]

"What If I Don't Know Anything?"

If it's true that every person you meet knows something you don't,[43] then the reverse must also be true. Every person you meet doesn't-know something *you* know! If I could still do mathematical proofs, I would put a bunch of impressive "if and only if" statements here. I can't do that anymore, so let's just assume I'm right.

Look at your résumé. What have you accomplished? What skills or knowledge did you gain in the process? Have you taken any classes, read any books, or completed any projects? If so, challenge yourself to impart this knowledge on someone else. No more excuses!

Start simple. Tweet an article to share with your professional network. Or recommend a good book, class, or podcast. Just like that, you've shared some new-found knowledge!

**Everyone knows enough
to be a mentor to someone.**
#NetworkBeyondBias

Be (A Little) Selfish

There are 7 billion altruistic reasons to be a mentor: one for each person on the planet. In case you're not motivated by do-gooderism, I've compiled more than a dozen *completely selfish* reasons to sign up to be a mentor:

✓ Gain confidence
✓ Build an industry talent pipeline
✓ Discover new strengths
✓ Build new skills for your resume
✓ Learn from your protégé
✓ Expand your professional network
✓ Find content for your blog
✓ Recognize your unique areas of expertise
✓ Remind yourself how far you've come
✓ Gain a new perspective on your own work and career
✓ Help peers fill open positions
✓ Learn about barriers to entry that may exist for your profession, industry, or company
✓ Helping others increases your own happiness[44]
✓ Leave a professional legacy
✓ Compound your own success
✓ Be seen as a leader among your peers

Whether your reasons are selfish or altruistic, someone needs you! Make this the year you expand your influence through new mentoring relationships.

WHERE CAN YOU MENTOR?

- Your own company (contact your HR department)

- Employee Resource Groups within your company (See Chapter 24)
- Professional associations within your industry (See Chapter 18)
- Toastmasters International
- High schools, colleges, or trade schools
- Prisons and juvenile detention facilities
- Formal mentoring organizations like American Corporate Partners
- Big Brothers Big Sisters, YMCA, and other community programs
- Your place of worship and other faith-based programs
- Youth sports organizations

PART FOUR: DIVERSE PERSPECTIVES

"We cannot solve our problems with the same thinking that created them."
– Albert Einstein

CHAPTER 17.
SEEK DIVERSE PERSPECTIVES ON PURPOSE

You've probably heard that "your network is your net worth."[45] Let's think about that for a moment. Your network is an investment, like your 401(k). You wouldn't put your life savings into just one company's stock. Nor would you pick your investment portfolio based on where your friends or cousins or sorority sisters work. You would diversify. In other words, you would spread your money around so that a downturn in a single company or industry wouldn't leave you bankrupt. You might even rebalance your portfolio occasionally so future investments didn't get too concentrated in a single stock or fund.

---

network, *noun*, an association of individuals having a common interest, formed to provide mutual assistance, helpful information, or the like[46]

DIVERSIFY YOUR NETWORK INVESTMENT

Just as you wouldn't put all your financial eggs in one basket, you also need to diversify your professional relationships. Your network, after all, is an investment of your time, your energy, and your reputation. Everything you will accomplish in your career will come from investing these resources effectively, efficiently, and wisely.

The returns on this investment include access to jobs and promotions, market insights, industry knowledge, clients, mentors, business partners, and so on. The interest you will compound in your network will make you valuable beyond your wildest dreams.

So why, then, do we concentrate our professional networks based on what's easiest, closest, or most like us? And if we're doing the work anyway, why not build our networks with diversity in mind? We need to recognize which perspectives we may be missing, and then we need to *seek out people who are different.*

Don't concentrate your professional network based on who is easiest, closest, or most like you.
#NetworkBeyondBias

In "The Bizarro Jerry" episode of the iconic sitcom *Seinfeld*, Elaine finds a new friend group that mirrors the show's main characters.[47] When George asks if he can join them, Elaine says, "I'm sorry...we already have a George." How many of *your* relationships are simply mirror images of other relationships? People in the same industry, from the same schools, living in the same area, and so on? All of those relationships are valuable, to be sure, but how much *additional* value could you accrue by seeking out people who are different?[48]

ASPECTS OF DIVERSITY

Different aspects of our identities radiate from us like spokes of a bicycle tire. The primary aspects are relatively immutable characteristics. These identifiers are the ones we and others use to determine how we fit into the world, at our very core: gender, race, age, generation, ethnicity, physical ability, primary language, nationality, and sexual orientation.[49]

Beyond these core identities, there are other factors that influence how we interact with and experience the world around us. Where we live, how much money we make, how we worship, and marital status are some examples. In terms of work, we might consider a person's industry, level of education, employer, or level of management as important diversity considerations.

> **Invest in people and ideas outside your own norms to create new opportunities for yourself and others.**
> **#NetworkBeyondBias**

All these dimensions combine in exciting ways that make each person's worldview a unique kaleidoscope of perspective. When we mix these points of view together, we innovate in ways that are rich and colorful and exciting, far beyond that which we could ever conceive on our own. By investing our time and energy into connecting with people and ideas outside of our own norms, we create new opportunities for ourselves and others.

In the following chapters, we'll explore just a few of the many types of diversity. I selected these topics to illustrate how different types of diversity can impact your professional network. In many cases, the topics I chose also allow me to share my own stories or stories from my CHAMP Network. You can use these as examples when you craft your own authentic stories (see Chapter 29).

CHAPTER 18.
INDUSTRY

Having a diverse network includes connecting beyond your current industry. The first step in assembling your CHAMP network, after all, is to build relationships with your Customers, who almost always work in a different industry. When you network beyond your industry, you can make connections, see larger economic trends, and innovate. You can also build partnerships for vertical or horizontal expansion.

For example, if you work in plumbing, you may not naturally have contacts in the banking and finance industry. However, you may need to know whether home sales are on the rise, whether new businesses are attracted to your area, or which neighborhoods are being developed or renovated. Through a strong relationship with a local banker, you may be the first to learn about an up-and-coming neighborhood or office park. Most people rely on recommendations from friends and neighbors, so you could see tremendous growth of your business just by having a quarterly lunch with a local home or business lender.

INNOVATE

New ideas come from new places. Evaluating them requires you to get outside an echo chamber of people who only know what you know.

TRANSFERABLE SKILLS

Your next star hire might be working in a dead-end job in a different industry. Conversely, you probably have numerous transferable skills that make you attractive to companies outside your traditional area of expertise.

INDUSTRY OVERLAP

Think about how your industry is part of the larger economic picture, cultural landscape, or community ecosystem. The insurance industry, for example, affects every other industry, and vice versa. What other industries affect your work? Which industries stand to gain or lose by changes that directly affect your company?

Information technology, human resources, training and development, management, consulting, and other industries are often embedded within companies whose focus is elsewhere. Similarly, an HR consulting firm probably has an information technology department.

As another example, consider a company that provides nurses with on-the-job technical training for medical devices. Would that company be part of the training industry, the nursing industry, the medical device industry, or the consulting industry? How might new training technologies or changes in nursing students' demographics affect this company? These are simple examples, but they illustrate the power of thinking beyond industry silos.

Better Understand Your Customers' Needs

Your Customers are focused on their own problems, challenges, markets, and opportunities. By better understanding those forces, you can serve your Customers more effectively.

See the Big Picture

If your industry lags others in technology, social trends, etc., you need to stay on top of what's coming. Has your company seen the impacts of wearable tech, bitcoin, and artificial intelligence? If not, you can network with people in industries that are leading the way. Learn from them how they've adapted, what lessons they've learned, and what opportunities they lost to their competitors. This allows you to think strategically by applying this knowledge within your own company or industry.

CREATE THE FUTURE

Is your company or industry a leader in trends and tech? If so, consider all the ways you could share what you've learned...and monetize it. Blogs, consulting gigs, speaking engagements, books, and e-courses on these topics could all create new revenue streams for your company.

CHAPTER 19.
AGE AND GENERATION

"The children now love luxury.
They have bad manners,
contempt for authority;
they show disrespect for elders
and love chatter in place of exercise."
– Socrates

Depending on your industry or company, you may already have four or five generations working side-by-side. Tremendous media attention is focused on how employers are scrambling to meet the needs of Millennials, now the largest generation in the workforce.[50] Baby Boomers still occupy top management spots in many companies. Meanwhile, members of the much smaller Generation X feel largely ignored. The impacts of Gen-Z remain to be seen.

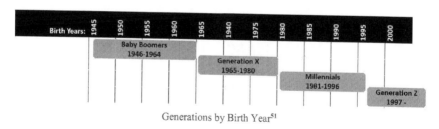

Generations by Birth Year[51]

Much of the conflict between generations is attributed to generational differences, and that certainly plays a role. Yet, I remember hearing my Baby Boomer parents talk about the cultural revolution taking place in the 1960s, when men started wearing their hair long and women started wearing pants to work. Their parents, my grandparents, initially scoffed at "men who look like women" and "women who dress like men." I see direct parallels between the counterculture movement of the 1960s and the Millennial and Gen Z trend toward gender-fluid identities. (More on this in Chapter 21.)

For most of us, it doesn't matter day-to-day whether the next generation is really revolutionary or we're simply repeating the patterns of the past. We still must find a way to work with and learn from one another if we want to contribute fully and realize our individual and collective potential. To me, that means recognizing that we were all young and full of new ideas when we entered the workforce. Yet we must also reckon with our obsession for youth, lest we be someday be victims of our own prejudices against older workers.

THE AGE DISCRIMINATION EPIDEMIC

Age discrimination is gaining more attention in the media, as Baby Boomers' influence in the workplace is dwindling. Millennials now comprise the largest segment of the workforce. Just about anyone over 50 will tell you that it's tough to compete with tech-savvy, confident 20-somethings who know how to negotiate wages, benefits, and company culture. During several recent conversations within and around my Associate Network, the topic of age discrimination has been dominant. For Baby Boomers who consider themselves "mid-career professionals," job security, health insurance coverage, and financial stability are significant concerns.

The author of the following essay wishes to remain anonymous. I take that trust seriously, and I am happy to have a platform for this story to be told, as it is a common problem for Baby Boomers in my network.

Facing Age Discrimination in a Job Interview

The interview was, in my opinion, proceeding well. I had done my research about the role and associated responsibilities. I was asking as many questions of the hiring manager as the hiring manager was asking of me. My skills matched what the hiring manager expected the ideal candidate to possess. It seemed like a mutual respect had been established in a short time frame. In an instant, though, all that changed – all because of one question: "How long do you think you'll continue to work?"

Thinking that I had somehow misunderstood, I asked, "Could you repeat that question for me?"

"Yes. How long do you think you'll continue to work?"

Thoughts flew through my mind as anger swelled up to the surface. Waves of anger, in fact. It took me time to tamp down the anger and become composed. I decided I could not answer the question.

There was a long period of silence. My answer finally came out, "I refuse to answer that question." I knew that I had just ensured the chances for landing the job were nil. Even if I had answered the question with a time frame, my odds would have only slightly improved. Why? Because it was apparent the hiring manager had determined I was of the age where I would presumably retire within the next five to ten years. It was equally clear this hiring manager was hesitant to take a chance on a worker who may retire in the not-so-distant future. I had run up against age bias regarding older workers in the workforce.

It is important to note I recognize the situation as age bias specifically targeting older workers. I also acknowledge there is age bias regarding younger workers. Think about all the quips one hears, ranging from someone is a "dinosaur" (older worker age bias) to being a "newbie" (younger worker age bias).

Age Discrimination Is Illegal in the United States

So, age bias is age bias, right? Not so much. A web search for "age discrimination in the workplace" yields 510,000 results. You can find scores more by varying the verbiage in your web search. Nearly all of these articles and news items deal with age bias against older workers, defined as workers 40 and above, consistent with the Age Discrimination in Employment Act of 1967 (29 U.S.C. § 631).[52,53] Gosselin and Tobin, authors of "Cutting 'Old Heads' at IBM"[54] provide detailed documentation and research suggesting a pattern of targeting older, highly paid, well performing employees at IBM from 2012 through 2017. Older workers, it seems, may indeed be facing more age bias than younger workers.

But it doesn't have to be this way. As a hiring manager myself, I see my job as finding the right person for any open position. I acknowledge and address any biases I may have about the "ideal" candidate in order to ensure no candidate is overlooked because of my biases. Recently I have asked recruiters to scrub resumes of dates so I don't try to figure out how old the applicant is or how long an applicant has been in a certain position. My experience with this approach has been positive, as a more diverse group of applicants ends up in the interview pool. It benefits not only me but my organization as I do find the right person for the position.

I challenge other hiring managers to examine their biases and find ways to give all applicants a fair chance. Had the hiring manager cited above done so, I may have gotten the job. As it stands, I am happy not to have been selected after such a question.

THIS ISSUE WILL AFFECT US ALL, EVENTUALLY

As a member of Generation X, I anticipate the large populations of Millennial and Gen-Z workers pose an imminent threat to my own career longevity. As such, I am seeking to educate myself now so I have enough runway to manage the risk. I'm curious as to how my contemporaries see themselves "aging out of the workforce." How will *we* manage the gap between our last day on the job and retirement? There are no easy answers, to be sure. Yet we must all prepare for this eventuality, and the sooner, the better.

CHAPTER 20.
GENDER

In my research for this chapter on gender, one point surprised me as being the hallmark of professional women: waiting until we're experts before taking on a new role.[55] While men tend to apply for a job when they meet 60 percent of the stated criteria, women will only apply if they can check off every item on the list.[56]

This reminded me of a conversation I had with a former [male] colleague who had taken a huge career risk. He took a significant *demotion* so he could get exposure in areas completely outside his experience and comfort zone. I literally gasped! How did he know he could be successful if he changed businesses, business functions, roles, and geographic scope – all at the same time?!? The question I asked was **"How did you become so fearless?"**

> **Don't wait until you think you're an expert before taking on a new role.**
> #NetworkBeyondBias

PROFESSIONAL WOMEN: DON'T UNDERCUT YOUR OWN VALUE

I used to take an 80/20 approach to job changes. If the new job was 80 percent stuff I knew how to do and 20 percent stuff I needed to learn, then it was probably a good (*read*: safe) opportunity for me. I've even coached other professional women to follow this approach, when they've come to me wondering if they should take a chance in their own careers. I remember several of them nodding and saying, "that seems like a safe approach." If my advice gave them the courage to try something new, then I'm glad I was able to give them a boost.

Looking back, I wish I'd taken a broader, transferable-skills view for myself and for those who sought my counsel. My new goal is to take a 50/50 approach using the same criteria above. Eventually, I may get to 20/80, taking my cue from the most daring men I know. I will go further by encouraging other professional women to do the same.

Women Apologize...Constantly

I've noticed that in meetings, women tend to contribute to the discussion by saying, "I don't know much about this, but...." or by starting with "This is probably a stupid question, but..." Please, please, please, don't tell people you're stupid.

Instead, consider why you were invited to the meeting in the first place. What perspective do you offer that no one else brings to the table? If you feel you *must* couch your comment or question in context, use it as an opportunity to remind yourself – and others – of your value to the group.

For example, "In my experience with this, I learned ... I see some similarities to this situation that I think are worth discussing," or "I have the benefit of looking at this with a fresh perspective, so can you explain why X is so important?"

Uptalk

Uptalk is my least favorite cultural phenomenon of late. Uptalk is the vocal intonation used by English-speakers to indicate that a sentence is a question. However, it has become more and more common for women to use uptalk for declarative statements as well, which results in us sounding less confident and less knowledgeable. In addition to explicitly apologizing for what we don't know (see above), we also use uptalk to implicitly apologize for having answers!

---

uptalk, *noun*, a manner of speaking in which declarative sentences are uttered with rising intonation at the end, as if they were questions.[57]

In fact, the more knowledgeable women are, the more likely they are to use uptalk to appear less threatening or less assertive. There is science to back this up. A William & Mary sociologist studied contestant responses on *Jeopardy!* The study showed that as women were more successful on the show, they were more likely to use uptalk. The opposite was true of male contestants.[58,59]

I recently read the autobiography of transgender professor and novelist Jennifer Finney Boylan.[60] In the memoir, Boylan writes that once she started living as a woman, she started using uptalk more often. Even when she introduced herself, she heard herself say, "My name is Jennifer?"

Fellow professional women, we have to stop ourselves and others from questioning everything we say as it's coming out of our mouths!

Moving Forward Together

I encourage both professional women and the men who support us to hold each other accountable for risk-taking and career success. Use specific constructive feedback to redirect limiting behaviors. Use specific positive feedback to reinforce effective ones.

Managers, please coach the women on your teams so they are not artificially limiting their own success. Understand your own biases and take steps to overcome them. Let's all work to ensure that we're treating ourselves with the same level of respect that we expect from others!

MEN: DON'T UNDERCUT PROFESSIONAL WOMEN, EITHER

Do you frequently travel alone? If so, you've probably had any number of "single-serving" conversations with the person next to you on the plane. It's what people do when we can't manage to avoid eye contact. Sometimes those conversations are a wonderful surprise. On my way to a speaking engagement, for example, the gentleman in the adjacent seat asked about my conference tote bag. As we traded introductions, I learned that he was a management executive building a new practice area for his firm. I added him to my LinkedIn network the moment we landed. Maybe even helped a friend get his next job. This is why I'm on the planet. Sweet!

On the return trip, I was in a middle seat. A woman with her adorable baby sat on the aisle. The gentleman on the other side of me (we'll call him Window Seat Guy) was starting to doze before the cabin door was even closed. Behind on my MBA coursework, I reached for the ridiculously heavy textbook in my carry-on tote bag. I expected to be asleep by paragraph four.

About three minutes in, Window Seat Guy asked why I was reading an accounting textbook. "Economics," I corrected. He informed me that marginal cost and marginal revenue are accounting concepts. Okay, but it's an Economics textbook. Says so right on the cover. I didn't argue, because there was no point.

Window Seat Guy seemed to be looking for a conversation, so I explained that I'm pursuing my MBA to complement my IT background. He asked how I liked Econ. I told him I find the material interesting conceptually, but (my apologies to the author) the textbook puts me to sleep. We talked awhile longer.

What Window Seat Guy learned about me as we talked:

- My second Bachelor's degree was in computer science
- My job responsibilities included managing global IT projects at a Fortune 100 company
- I have a passion for leadership development, have launched my own company, and am authoring two books (one of which you are reading now)
- I was headed home from a conference where I had spoken to college professors about inclusive networking
- I'm early in my MBA program and preferred the Finance class to the Economics course

I learned similar tidbits about Window Seat Guy's professional background and the nature of his business trip. It turns out Window Seat Guy is the Chief Financial Officer of a technology startup.

And Then It Happened...

It was *after* all of this that he gave me what he must have considered to be sage advice from a seasoned accounting professional:

> *"You might understand economics better if when the book says oil and gas, you think in terms of purses and shoes."*
> – Window Seat Guy

Many thoughts went through my mind, none of which I felt I should vocalize in the moment. Instead, I simply offered, "Or, I could think in terms of oil and gas."

Why Is This Still Happening?

This is the same kind of nonsense I dealt with twenty years ago when I got my Computer Science degree. I knew then it was because I was a woman, but figured my youth also played in. It's easy to want to give advice to young people. Now that I'm older, I catch myself doing it all the time. (I'll work on that.) I'm in my 40s, for crying out loud. (See? Young people don't say "for crying out loud" yet.) *When do I finally get to be taken seriously as a hard-working, experienced professional?*

Window Seat Guy is some company's CFO. How does he talk to the women in his department? What assumptions is he making about them? How long will they stay? Does he know why they all probably hate working for him?

ENOUGH ALREADY

We all need to stop assuming women are superficial know-nothings who can't process complex information. If you are a leader in your company, realize that microaggressions (see Chapter 28) hurt the productivity, engagement, and longevity of your workforce. Not because women and people of color are less educated (we aren't) or have fewer qualifications (we don't). But because we are tired of others' inability to see us as intellectual and professional equals. We deserve much, much better than to have to repeatedly explain our capabilities and value to people like Window Seat Guy.

WHAT TO DO INSTEAD: A MODEL FOR MALE LEADERS

When Scott Woolgar was my manager fifteen years ago, he pushed me beyond my limited self-image. I saw myself as a junior-level software developer; he saw my potential to be a leader. He simultaneously saw the big picture, the minutest details, and everything in between. He taught me how to look in different directions, how to see things I hadn't previously noticed. He kept me on my toes with his ability to see me as I *could* be and to hold me accountable to a higher standard. He believed in me before I did, *and he told me so.*

Scott empowered me to fire on all cylinders, despite the dysfunctional company around us. He made it safe for me to take initiative, to point out problems, to try something completely new, to lead others, to travel around the world, and to stand up for myself. He prepared me for my first management role, then recommended me for the position. When I floundered as a new leader, he told me to call him for support any time I needed it. And he did all of this from within the most toxic work environment I've ever experienced. Had I gone through that time with anyone else as my manager, it would have left me broken. But I came out of it strong and ready for everything that has happened since.

Last year, I consulted Scott about my desire to take my career in an entirely new direction. He has once again become my mentor:

encouraging, sincere, and helpful. He nudges me in the right direction without making me feel like I've made a mistake. He takes the time to tell me specifically what I'm doing right so I can keep doing it. Because of the respect I have for him, I always take his words to heart.

Once again, I'm forced to believe in myself simply because I trust his judgment. Sometimes I need to borrow courage, other times I need to know the next step. He's made me better – in big ways and small ways – every single time I've talked with him. Most importantly, Scott has never let me believe anything that isn't true about my capabilities or my limitations, and he's never asked for anything in return.

NETWORK BEYOND BIAS

CHAPTER 21.
GENDER IDENTITY: A PRIMER FOR PEOPLE WHO JUST DON'T GET IT

In most Western cultures, gender is paramount to individuals' identities and how we interact with one another. Before a baby is even born, we ask, "Is it a boy or a girl?" The newborn receives pink dresses or blue blankets, and this is only the beginning of their gender-coded socialization. Many of us accept this boy-or-girl framework as a simple fact of life, the result of a coin flip that can only end in "heads or tails." But for millions of people, male and female gender identities are neither mutually exclusive (separate and distinct) nor exhaustive (covering all possibilities). If this is a new concept for you, you are not alone.

Gender identity conversations used to leave me confused and uncomfortable. Nevertheless, I have always tried to raise my children with a conscious rejection of traditional gender stereotypes. For example, my oldest son got dolls for Christmas when he asked for them. My youngest son didn't get dolls because he never asked for them. Dinner conversations included frank discussions about how boys and girls are sometimes treated differently. We have always talked openly about love being what makes a family, regardless of who lives in or outside of someone's household. We even talked about how hard it must be for someone to feel like a boy on the inside and look like a girl on the outside, or vice versa.

Yet, despite my ability to mostly say the right words, I still struggled to understand transgender and nonbinary identities. Finally, I had an epiphany. It isn't my job to understand or validate someone else's identity. My responsibility involves accepting people as they are and respecting each person's unique experience. I was, at long last, on a path of being a genuine ally to the trans and nonbinary community.

My journey toward being a *vocal* trans ally started with a Facebook post in 2017, shortly after I attended a gala for the Human Rights Campaign in Boston:

"I've never been around very many 'out' transgender people. Tonight I met several of them. I want you to know...you can't 'tell' who they are. And even if you can, be respectful. These folks have faced more hardship than most of us can imagine... Please, for the love of humanity, just be a decent person.... Seriously, if a 40-year-old woman from Southern Indiana can work this out...So. Can. You."

A few days later, I got a call from someone I had known for decades but with whom I hadn't spoken in several years. "I'm trans," they said, "and you're the first person I've told other than my therapist." For them to have lived with this lifelong truth, without support from friends and family, with the constant fear of being discovered must have been overwhelming. I'm embarrassed I couldn't have come out as an ally sooner to provide my friend with the support they needed. I'm saddened that my clumsy allyship was the best my friend could find in their network. Since that time, I've worked to educate myself on the issues transgender and nonbinary individuals face. The statistics are heartbreaking.

GENDER IDENTITY ISSUES: BY THE NUMBERS

There are an estimated 1.4 million transgender adults in the United States.[61] While there are no official records, independent studies have estimated anywhere from 2,150 to 15,500 transgender individuals serve in the U.S. armed forces.[62]

Only twenty states and the District of Columbia protect trans people from discrimination in employment[63] and housing.[64] This means that in 30 states, trans people have *no legal remedy* if they are fired or evicted because they are trans. Perhaps that explains why trans women are four times more likely to live in extreme poverty (less than $10,000 annually) than the general population.[65]

Only sixteen states and D.C. recognize violence targeting trans people as a hate crime.[66] Yet, 2016 and 2017 saw consecutive records for the number of trans people murdered.[67] Trans people are also subject to high rates of abuse,[68] harassment,[69] and arrest.[70]

Anti-trans discrimination takes a significant personal toll. More than 40 percent of trans people will attempt suicide in their lifetimes, and those rates increase when trans people also suffer disadvantages due to race, education, income, homelessness, or being victims of violence.[71] Nonbinary people have the highest rates of suicide and attempted suicide of any identity group.[72]

TERMINOLOGY

For those unfamiliar with gender identity concepts, here's a quick vocabulary lesson.

Assigned gender – the gender initially proclaimed at an individual's birth (typically male, female, or intersex)

Intersex – someone whose physical manifestation of gender falls outside of or between medical guidelines for what is considered male or female

Gender identity – the gender with which an individual identifies (typically male, female, or nonbinary)

Nonbinary – a gender identity that is neither male nor female

Gender expression – the way an individual presents their gender identity (typically masculine, feminine, or androgynous)

Androgynous – a gender expression that is neither exclusively masculine nor exclusively feminine

Cisgender – someone whose gender identity matches the gender they were assigned at birth. Avoid using the terms "normal," "real man," or "real woman" to describe cisgender people. The term "privileged" is acceptable, however (wink!).

Transgender, or trans – someone whose gender identity differs from the gender they were assigned at birth. Trans men, for example, are people who identify as male but who were not identified as male at birth. *Avoid using the terms "transsexual" or "cross-dressing" to describe trans people. Transsexual* is an outdated term that originated in the medical field. *Cross-dressing* refers to people who wear clothing outside of traditional gender norms, usually as a form of gender expression.[73]

121

Gender confirmation – a complicated and lengthy medical process whereby a person's physicality is altered to match their gender identity. *Avoid using the term "sex change," which ignores the individual's identity by overemphasizing only the physical manifestations of gender.*[74]

Transition – the process of changing one's gender identity and/or gender expression, regardless of whether one undertakes the gender confirmation process. *Again, avoid using the term "sex change."*

Gender fluidity – the notion that a person's gender identity or gender expression is not fixed

Gender nonconforming –a catch-all term for gender-fluid and nonbinary individuals, and sometimes for individuals who choose a gender expression that violates societal norms

Genderqueer – a term more often used by young, gender nonconforming people, and particularly people of color; this term carries an additional connotation of political activism. *Avoid describing someone as "queer" (adjective) unless you know for sure an individual self-describes that way. Never use the word "queer" as a noun. For many older people, the word "queer" has been used to demean, degrade, and dehumanize them. However, some people – predominantly Millennials and Gen Zers (See Chapter 19) – have chosen to empower themselves by reclaiming the word "queer."*

LGBTQ – Lesbian, Gay, Bisexual, Transgender, and Queer [Community]; multiple variations of this acronym exist.

QUESTIONS TO AVOID

If you're not male or female, then what are you? Just as some people are more feminine or more masculine or neither or both, and just as some people are taller or shorter or somewhere in between, many people experience their gender along a continuum. **Try instead,** *"What are your preferred pronouns?"*

How do you know? / Are you sure? / What if you're wrong? Any time a person is facing a tremendous amount of resistance to be themselves, assume that they know what they're talking about. They've done more research, had more conversations, and spent more sleepless nights trying to work this out than you can imagine. **Try instead,** *"How can I support you?"*

What's your real name? / What did you look like before? / Any questions about biology, physiology, or emotional trauma. **Try instead,** "It's a pleasure meeting you."

Have you had the surgery? There's not just one surgery, and surgical procedures are only a fraction of what's involved in a medical transition. Most important, though, is that what's going on under another person's undergarments is almost never any of your business. **Try instead,** *literally anything else.*

WAYS TO SHOW RESPECT TO INDIVIDUALS

Getting someone's name right is usually your first opportunity to demonstrate respect. **Use an individual's preferred name**, and ensure you are pronouncing it correctly. Ask as many times as you need to get it right. Write it down if necessary. This is a good rule to follow, not just for interacting with trans individuals, but when networking with anyone!

Use each person's preferred pronouns. This can be tricky, especially if the pronouns are new to you. If you mess up, apologize and try again. When in doubt, ask. You are also usually safe using they / them / their. Never, ever, ever use "it" to refer to a person, and never, ever, ever make someone's identity the subject of ridicule, whether they can hear you or not. Dehumanizing people is never respectful, never appropriate, and never inclusive.

Keep in mind that some people may present themselves differently in different environments. For example, one nonbinary individual I know (pronouns: *ve, vim, vir*) presents as female and uses vir legal name and the pronouns she/her/hers at work, because ve fears the repercussions of being out professionally. The same individual presents as nonbinary and uses a masculine name in vir personal life. Take your cues from the individual, and ask if you're unsure.

Do not "out" anyone as trans or nonbinary. Use each person's preferred name and pronouns, and leave it at that. Remember, for many trans and nonbinary individuals, being outed can threaten their safety, their income, their housing arrangements, and their health.

DISRUPT THE GENDER BINARY

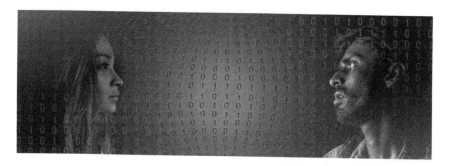

Introduce your pronouns when you introduce yourself. For example, when I meet someone new, I could say, "Hi, I'm Amy C. Waninger. My pronouns are she, her, and hers." Specifying your pronouns helps normalize differences and helps to challenge assumptions that people may have. At networking events, put your pronouns on your name tag. "My Name Is" stickers are boring anyway, and now you have a built-in conversation starter. Update your social network profiles (such as Facebook, Twitter, and LinkedIn) and your email signature to include your pronouns.

Ask people for their pronouns, particularly if you have already shared your own. Don't assume, based on someone's appearance, that you know which pronouns they prefer. While worrying about pronouns may be new to you (remember the definition of *privilege* from Chapter 5), there are many people for whom pronouns are a constant source of frustration and dehumanization. Making a heartfelt effort will go a long way toward building trust in your relationships.

Avoid stereotyping behaviors, inanimate objects, or emotions as "girly," "manly," "feminine," or "masculine." Avoid chastising children for showing an interest in something traditionally associated with a different gender. Don't use "like a girl" as a criticism or "for a girl" as a compliment. I once challenged a day care provider who told me she had to keep taking dolls away from one of the preschool boys. We got into a lengthy conversation about why that was important to her, especially when she let the girls play with toys traditionally associated with boys, like trucks and blocks.

BECOME AN ACTIVE ALLY

Educate yourself by reading memoirs by or biographies and articles about trans people. Jennifer Finney Boylan (author and professor) has published at least two memoirs about her life as a trans woman. There are numerous articles about successful trans businesswomen like Laverne Cox (actor, producer, and activist), Martine Rothblatt (lawyer, author, entrepreneur), and Vivienne Ming (scientist & entrepreneur). Memoirs from Brian Belovitch and Jay Sennett offer first-person trans male perspectives. Famous trans men are a little more difficult to find. Chaz Bono is one notable exception.

You can also watch TED Talks by Alice Miller, Geena Rocero, Valentijn De Hingh, Fox Fisher, and others. Listening to personal stories – and seeing the real people behind them – can have a profound impact on your understanding and empathy.

If you design computer systems, paper registration forms, or other registration and identification processes, allow individuals to self-identify beyond the traditional labels of "male" and "female." Include options such as nonbinary, transgender, or simply "other" so that everyone feels they can answer the question honestly. Bonus points if you can provide space for the individual to list their pronouns!

Finally, speak up if you witness someone being disrespectful (see Chapter 28). Your example and presence can go a long way toward helping someone feel safe. You may even help someone else question their own prejudices.

CHAPTER 22.
SEXUAL ORIENTATION

Earlier in 2018, I committed to out myself to over 50,000 people, almost entirely at once, as part of an education initiative at a Fortune 100 company. In truth, I had made my decision nearly a year prior and was just waiting to be asked!

I don't go out of my way to hide my sexual orientation. As a bisexual, though, the opposite is almost always true: I have to go so far out of my way to be seen that I typically don't bother. After all, I'm a working mother, married to an amazing man. People assume I'm straight. Just as, if I were a working mother, married to an amazing woman, they would assume I was a lesbian. My identity as a bisexual is constant. My visibility as a member of the LGBTQ community is another matter.

When my employer's LGBTQ Employee Resource Group (ERG) launched, I got involved right away. I posted messages of support on the company intranet. I sent thank you notes to ERG and corporate leaders. Although the ERG's focus at that time was concentrated on employees and events at the company's headquarters, I kept showing up to meetings, pushing for more programs for the Midwest, where I felt we had a significant need for education, advocacy, and home office support. I became as involved as possible, coordinating our first-ever entry in the Indy Pride parade (and our second-ever entry, for that matter). I attended ERG leadership meetings, planning events, and even a very fancy East Coast gala.

It wasn't long before other ERG leaders complimented my "allyship." Despite my passion and persistence, they didn't see me as part of their tribe. I didn't know if I should correct them or just say "thank you." I felt like such a fraud as I struggled to be out at work – even within the Pride ERG!

To be fair, my experience with coming out as bisexual has always been a stressful one. Many gay men and lesbians have told me bisexuality doesn't really exist. Many straight people have told me bisexuality is deviant and hedonistic. People, both gay and straight, tend to assume that I'm confused, attention-seeking, or "being political." They ask awkward questions like, "So...how does that work, exactly?"

For those thinking this only happens in the Midwest, think again. I've had these conversations in Indiana, sure, but also in New York, Massachusetts, and California. In my personal life, as a working professional, and *even at LGBTQ events*, I am almost always compelled to address damaging stereotypes about my marital fidelity and mental health.

Many people tell me my identity is not relevant. Well-meaning people tell me I should keep it to myself, *even when it feels dishonest to do so.* I am told to step back into the closet, as though my identity and lived experience were shameful or imaginary.

But in April 2017, I attended the Out Women in Business conference, a one-day gathering of professional LGBTQ women and nonbinary individuals. This event triggered a turning point in my career. In one session, Out Leadership's Stephanie Sandberg presented a "supermodel slideshow" in which she highlighted a series of lesbian and trans women business leaders around the world. Then she told us about Inga Beale, the CEO of Lloyd's of London.

What got my attention was not that Ms. Beale and I worked in the same industry. It was the fact that she is an out, bisexual woman – who happens to be married to a man. In her experience, colleagues were more accepting of her after she married her husband than they were when she was in a prior relationship with a woman. Feeling that she should be accepted on her own terms, and not as a function of her partner's gender at any point in time, she decided to be more visible. By forcing the conversation, she makes a conscious effort to shed some of her privilege. In doing so, she makes the world a little safer for people like me.

For the first time in my professional life, I had a role model for being honest about myself to others. It is hard to overstate the impact of seeing someone like me who made it. All the way to the CEO spot.

In a conservative industry, no less! I resolved then that I would no longer "keep to myself" about who I am. Because I, too, want to make this journey easier for the next person, and the next, until we can all be easily seen. So when young people look for role models, they can see themselves in us.

After my "coming out" blog post went live within the company, several people responded with supportive comments. Some shared how they had similarly struggled to come out. Others acknowledged that they had been reluctant to accept others' identities. Many thanked me publicly for creating a space for them to reflect on or relate to my story. What was most touching for me, though, were those who contacted me privately to say that they are still closeted at home or at work, still looking for the chance to be accepted fully by friends and colleagues. I long for the day when we can all be loved and valued, and for many of us, it cannot come soon enough.

If you seek to be an ally to the LGBTQ community, speak up. If you admire the courage it takes to come out at work, say so. Don't delete your sister's wife or your uncle's boyfriend from your family's stories or speak about them in hushed tones. Your LGBTQ colleagues are constantly watching you to see if you'll supportive or hostile to them. When someone does come out to you, ask simply, "How can I support you?" Then, give them the support they have asked for. That's what makes you a true ally.

CHAPTER 23.
RACE & ETHNICITY

In the United States, few words are more polarizing than "race" and "racism." Yet, Americans suffer from constant racial tension, race-based economic disparities, and institutionalized racism. If we are to change this, White Americans must listen to people whose experiences and perspectives could inform and enlighten us. Our blindness to our own privilege is oppressive. Our sense of entitlement is embarrassing.

No single book can begin to untangle this topic. This one merely attempts to offer some steps in the right direction.

SO CLOSE, AND YET SO FAR

My first undergraduate degree was in Criminal Justice, with minor concentrations in Sociology and Spanish. I was one course shy of a second major in African-American Studies. I loved reading Richard Wright's novels, Maya Angelou's poetry, and Dr. King's speeches. For the first time in my life, history seemed to be a story about people and their experiences, rather than endless lists of names and dates to be memorized and regurgitated.

Yet, despite an almost insatiable desire to understand the history, contributions, and perspectives of African-Americans, I know *so little* about race in America. In fact, the great tragedy is that I didn't learn how to be an ally to people of color as a result of my studies. I thought, in my youth, that I had checked all the right boxes to speak with authority on racism. I had no understanding of how ignorant and arrogant I was being.

DAMAGE DONE

Now, to be fair, my youthful arrogance and lack of empathy were indiscriminate. But where those character flaws overlapped with my racial (or any other) privilege was especially damaging to the people around me. I am embarrassed and ashamed for all the times I was – and probably continue to be – ignorant of my impact. Despite my best intentions and attempts to educate myself, I am certain I will continue to make mistakes. By being careful, cognizant, reflective, and observant, I can make fewer mistakes and ones that are less severe.

THE BASICS

For white people whose friendship circles and work relationships are overwhelmingly, or perhaps exclusively, white, here are some first steps:

1. Get to know people of color by cultivating friendships with people from different backgrounds. Build each relationship slowly over time, and be intentional about being inclusive.

2. Avoid saying that you're "colorblind" or "don't see race." Race and ethnicity are important components of an individual's identity and are central to their experience of the world. Many times white people avoid mentioning race or ethnicity at all or downplay its importance in an effort to avoid appearing racist.

3. Don't ask people of color to speak for their entire race or ethnic group. Realize that all demographic groups have as many nuances as your own in-group, rather than a single monolithic, shared identity.

> **Avoid saying that you're
> "colorblind" or "don't see race."**
> #NetworkBeyondBias

One of my Associates, Sabrina Bristo, MSW, gives a great example of a true friend and ally from her own experience:

> One of my closest friends from college (undergraduate studies) is a white woman from San Francisco. We became friends because she is very comfortable talking about race and inequality. She went to a Historically Black College/University (HBCU) because the tuition was affordable. But she was already comfortable being around very diverse groups. That's the kind of relationship building

and cultural humility that fosters understanding, which most white people never really experience.

MY WAY FORWARD

Perhaps you've already conquered the basics. In that case, I hope you'll join me in and hold me accountable for my commitments to continue on this journey. Specifically, I will:

- Help others feel safe in my presence by standing up for them when necessary
- Avoid engaging in microaggressions (More on this in Chapter 28) and intervene when I observe them. Speak up when anyone makes a racist comment or joke, whether overt or subtle, regardless of the audience or the power dynamics at play
- Listen to people of color without judgment, defensiveness, or denying their experiences
- Amplify the voices, stories, and concerns of people of color without speaking for them
- Notice when people of color are excluded from a discussion, a decision, or an opportunity, and do what I can to include them
- Pay attention to whether people of color seek me out as a mentor, partner, or ally, and look within myself if they do not
- Continue to educate myself about the history, contributions, challenges and oppression of these communities

- Think critically and contextually about racial bias in the media, institutional racism, and the pervasiveness of white supremacy / primacy in American culture
- Constantly declare my *desire* to be an ally and act accordingly
- Wait to have the *title* of "ally" bestowed upon me by others before I consider claiming it for myself

All of this combined may still be insufficient. When I fully understand the next steps in this journey, I hope I have the courage to commit to them.

Visit the website for links to additional resources for improving understanding across racial differences.

WWW.NETWORKBEYONDBIAS.COM

PART FIVE: EXPAND YOUR HORIZONS

"If you put yourself in a position where you have to stretch outside your comfort zone, then you are forced to expand your consciousness."
– Les Brown

CHAPTER 24.
EMPLOYEE RESOURCE GROUPS

The best place to start building your professional network is within your own company. (You can't stop there, of course, so networking outside your employer's "firewall" is covered in the following chapters.) You can easily connect with members of your own team or department, and you should absolutely do so. If you're new to a company, or if you work for a large organization, try to branch out into other divisions as well. One fantastic way to do this is through Employee Resource Groups.

WHAT ARE EMPLOYEE RESOURCE GROUPS (ERGs)?

Employee Resource Groups (ERGs) have started cropping up in companies. You may know them as *Employee Affinity Groups (EAGs), Business Resource Groups (BRGs), staff networks,* or by another name. These groups are usually launched to help employees, particularly those who face cultural headwinds, connect with one another. And there are many other benefits for companies and employees alike.

Employee Resource Group (ERG), *noun*, voluntary, employee-led groups that foster a diverse, inclusive workplace aligned with organizational mission, values, goals, business practices, and objectives[75]

BENEFITS TO COMPANIES

Finding and Attracting Diverse Talent

There is a significant talent shortage in many industries, and many companies struggle to meet aggressive recruiting goals. These companies may be in a rut: recruiting from the same professional networks, schools, or geographic areas for decades.

By tapping into the networks of current employees, companies can expand their reach to find and attract talent in areas they haven't approached before. People tend to know others who are similar to themselves. Companies can therefore find new pools of talent by leveraging the connections of employees from non-traditional backgrounds.

From a recruiting perspective, ERGs offer an attractive selling point to job candidates. Many new employees want to believe they will feel welcome and accepted in a new company. A company with ERGs can demonstrate cultural understanding and acceptance before the candidate has even applied for the job. Having an ERG tells the job candidate, "There are successful people in the company just like you. They want to help you be successful, too."

Introducing New Employees to the Corporate Culture

Once hired, new employees may need help understanding cultural norms of the company. Fellow ERG members may be helpful in this process, especially if the corporate culture does not readily translate to the subculture of the affinity group. For example, Asian-Americans may find it difficult to tout their own accomplishments due to values instilled in them since childhood.[76] Women may have been taught to downplay their intelligence in group settings.[77] In a large company, these professionals may need to find ways to adapt that are both advantageous in the workplace *and* culturally acceptable. ERGs can help provide integration strategies from a first-hand perspective.

Identifying and Retaining Top Talent

ERGs give a voice and sense of community to employees who may otherwise feel isolated or under-represented, helping companies to retain talent in their organizations. When people feel isolated, they are not as engaged. Connected employees are more productive, more loyal, and better brand ambassadors. Connected employees stick around.[78]

Connected employees stick around.
#NetworkBeyondBias

Rewards and recognition are also a key factor in employee retention. Rewards themselves can reflect the bias of managers and fail to create true employee incentives. If rewards overwhelmingly reflect the interests of a homogeneous management team, they are likely to appeal to only a narrow demographic within the company. A company that is fond of giving out golf packages as employee rewards, for example, may make employees with disabilities feel alienated. Public recognition for meeting or exceeding goals may drive high-performing Asian-Americans away. When companies consult with their ERGs about reward structures, they create more inclusive incentive programs, encouraging all employees to do their best.

Research shows that managers are more likely to reward and promote employees who are like them.[79] This is especially true when those managers don't recognize their own biases. If a company has a high percentage of managers with similar demographics, it is unlikely that those demographics will change over time. ERGs offer a different avenue for those managers to recognize talent they might otherwise overlook. They can also help mitigate against the default mode of hiring, recognizing, and promoting only within their existing inner circles.

Expanding into New Markets and Customer Segments

Breaking into new markets can be tricky. Many companies have struggled to set the right tone in their advertising. Others may not even recognize that they have a potential niche customer base. In a 2017 interview, Howard J. Ross reminded us that it's hard to sell to someone you've just insulted.[80] It's perhaps even harder to sell to someone you don't know exists.

> **It's hard to sell to someone**
> **when you don't know they exist.**
> **#NetworkBeyondBias**

A diverse employee base can give an insider perspective on different markets and customer preferences. For example, a Latinx ERG might help a company translate both the language and the "feel" of commercials so they seem natural to the target community.[81] An ERG for Lesbian, Gay, Bisexual, and Transgender (LGBT) employees may help a financial services company create new products or services tailored to the legal issues faced by this consumer group.[82] By working with management and marketing teams, ERGs can provide a competitive edge in market segments where the company has previously underperformed.

Latinx, *adjective*, a person of Latin American origin or descent (used as a gender-neutral or non-binary alternative to Latino or Latina)[83]

BENEFITS TO EMPLOYEES

Professional Development Opportunities

As companies seek to develop new talent pools, employees can use ERGs to position themselves for success. Participation in ERGs can provide opportunities that may be missing from the employee's "day job." For example, an employee who plans an ERG networking event gains project management experience. Another employee who attends the networking event may meet managers from other areas of the company. ERGs provide endless volunteer opportunities and chances to be noticed by management.

A Sense of Belonging

Most employees are happier and more engaged when they feel connected to others at work. ERGs can provide a sense of community and connection, even in very large companies. By meeting others with similar life experiences, people feel more supported. These relationships often go beyond transactional, into deep friendships and mentorships. Project work, problem solving, career management, and other daily realities of corporate life are much easier when you have strong relationships.

Address Ignorance and Stereotypes Head-on

Individual employees often find themselves on the receiving end of harmful stereotypes. Many will find that even well-meaning coworkers can be insensitive to or ignorant about deeply-held cultural norms. By themselves, they may be uncomfortable addressing or combating these situations. However, an ERG can organize entertaining "mythbusting" sessions, cultural awareness events, or expert panels that educate the larger corporate community. Doing so not only improves the environment for affinity employees. Everyone benefits from having a broader perspective and greater empathy.

---

stereotype, *noun*, a widely held but fixed and oversimplified image or idea of a particular type of person or thing[84]

Including Everyone in the Conversation

When you look at your company's executive team, do you see someone who looks like you? Do you see someone to whom you can easily relate? If so, you may take this representation for granted. At the end of the day, inclusion isn't about being "politically correct." Nor does it mean offering special treatment to certain groups of people. True inclusion requires recognition that certain interests and perspectives are represented by default. ERGs help expand the circle to include new perspectives at all levels of the organization.

Think about a time when you felt different: new kid in school, new on the job, dressed informally for a formal event, visiting a different office, visiting a foreign country. Can you imagine feeling that way *every day of your career?*

We can all benefit by educating ourselves on the experience of being different and by opening ourselves up to the value that experience offers. If we are at our most candid when we find ourselves in the majority, then we exhibit the greatest emotional intelligence when we are in the minority.

Get Involved as Soon as Possible!

If your company has ERGs, consider joining a group with which you identify. Especially in large companies, this can provide a sense of belonging that you may not even know you're missing.

Then, sign up as an **"ally"** in an ERG that is outside your own identity. If that makes you uncomfortable, ask yourself why – and be brave enough to answer yourself honestly. I hope you'll take a few minutes to learn more ... from a different perspective.

---

ally, *verb*, side with or support[85]

If your company doesn't offer ERGs yet, consider some alternatives. You could, for example, help start a mentoring program for new employees or set up networking luncheons for people across departments.

When you attend conferences, association meetings, or other events, find ways to include people who are still finding their place in the group. Or invite colleagues to join you at professional networking events.

Remember, everyone wants a chance to contribute, to do valuable work, and to belong to something bigger than themselves. In most cases, there is no shortage of work to be done. By including others, we maximize our own impact on the organizations, communities, and interests we serve.

> ## Leaders must be able to say, "I see you. I value you. You are welcome here."
> ### #NetworkBeyondBias

If you are a manager, provide visible and vocal support for your employer's ERGs, especially if your team members are involved in them. Seeing support among managers is powerful for employees. Manager support says, "I see you" to employees who worry they may be invisible. A manager's endorsement of an ERG says, "I value you" to employees who may have been made to feel "less than" in other companies. When you declare yourself an ally to an employee's ERG, you say to him or her, "You are welcome here. All of you." As managers, we must always be willing to say, "I see you. I value you. You are welcome here" to every person who joins our team.

Chapter 25.
TO THE INDUSTRY...
AND BEYOND!

Once you understand how important networking is to your career, you'll want to get started right away. Don't limit your CHAMP network to your own company, or even your own industry! Get out of your own backyard as often as possible by attending formal and informal networking events. Within each industry, there are countless opportunities for formal networking. Try to persuade your manager to sponsor your attendance or participation. Many conference websites even offer templates and sample letters to help you do so!

PROFESSIONAL ASSOCIATIONS

Professional associations are typically non-profit organizations that seek to advance the "state of the art" in an industry or field of practice. These associations usually offer training events, certifications, professional designations, conferences, and networking events to members and prospective members. Such offerings are typically hosted by chapters at the local, state, and national levels, so you can determine how involved you want to be. To find an association in your field, search the web for "_____ industry association" or "_____ industry certification." Be sure to include your specific industry in the search.

Many industries also have associations dedicated to diversifying the talent pool and advancing specific demographic groups within the industry. In the cybersecurity industry, for example, the International Consortium of Minority Cybersecurity Professionals (ICMCP) hosts multiple events annually and has an active online community. Organizations like the National Association of African Americans in Human Resources (NAAAHR) and the National Association of Women Lawyers (NAWL) strive to meet the needs of affinity members in their respective fields. If you don't identify with an organization's target demographic, find out if allies are welcome as members or guests at their events. Don't be afraid to show up at the conference that's not for you. The experience will be invaluable!

Vendor User Groups

Does your company use software or information services from outside vendors? Check the websites of the companies that provide these services. They often host their own conferences, user groups, and advisory panels so they can stay connected to their customers. Be sure to check with your manager before attending, as your company may have a policy about what level of involvement is appropriate.

INDUSTRY TRADE SHOWS

Going further, industry-wide trade shows bring together multiple vendors in one location. Your company may participate in some trade shows as a vendor and in others as a consumer of goods and services. Ask the salespeople in your company or industry about the trade shows they attend and see if you can tag along.

COLLEGES AND UNIVERSITIES

Colleges and universities in your area may host recruiting and networking events so students can meet with or learn from alumni and local professionals. Some of these events are specific to fields of study, others are not. Call your company's HR department or check the local campus's website to find these opportunities. Remember to ask how you can get involved with mentoring programs on campus as well!

Another way to make the most of your local campus (or an online program) is to take a class. During your studies, you'll have a chance to collaborate and connect with people of all different backgrounds and ages. At the same time, you'll build your own knowledge and skills, making you more valuable to your employer and your network!

TOASTMASTERS CLUBS

Membership in Toastmasters International is, in my opinion, the single best value in experiential learning. You can learn to speak in public, manage meetings, improve your listening skills, and develop leadership skills. In the process, you'll learn a lot about fellow club members, many of whom you would never have otherwise met. You expand your professional network while becoming more valuable within it!

MEETUPS AND COMMUNITY EVENTS

Connecting in your local community is always time well spent, as it allows you to meet people who have similar passions. Becoming a volunteer in a community organization helps you build skills and self-confidence as well. Check sites like Meetup.com or VolunteerMatch.org for local opportunities to reach out and give back.

SOCIAL MEDIA

Finally, and especially if you have mobility issues or significant time constraints, expand your network via social media. Join a Slack channel related to your field, industry, or interests. Engage with other professionals and thought leaders on Twitter. Scroll LinkedIn and comment on posts or articles that resonate with you. Contributing to discussions on these platforms can help you build both relationships and name recognition. I've personally used Twitter and LinkedIn to connect with thought leaders around the world, adding them to my own CHAMP Network over time.

"You can use social media to connect with thought leaders from around the world!" @AmyCWaninger #NetworkBeyondBias

CHAPTER 26.
STRETCH YOURSELF
– GO TO THE CONFERENCE
THAT'S NOT FOR YOU

When I travel, I use the opportunity to connect face-to-face with people from past work lives. This keeps me active and engaged with my CHAMP network, even when we don't have an immediate overlap of interests. I also love hearing what my friends are learning through new jobs, challenges, and relationships.

During one such trip, I scheduled coffee with a former colleague whom I greatly admire. Megan is smart, works with integrity, and leads with authenticity. On this occasion, Megan had just returned from a large conference for women in business. Her employer was a key corporate sponsor. I was looking forward to hearing her second-hand messages of empowerment and inclusion, so I asked about the conference right away.

PREACHING TO THE CHOIR

"It was great, but I got so angry," Megan said. My confusion must have been evident. She continued:

"I've been to this conference a few years in a row now. All these amazing women go on stage to talk about how difficult it is to be an ambitious woman in corporate America.

"They talk about work/life balance struggles. Someone gives statistics about how many women will get frustrated and leave the workforce to care for children or aging parents. They all use words like *resilience, empowerment,* and *determination.* There are stories about subtle sexism, blatant sexism, and sexual harassment. We hear how we won't close the pay gap or reach C-Suite gender equity in our lifetimes.

"And there we all sit: hundreds of women who have all experienced discrimination, harassment, sexism, pay inequality. WE. ALREADY. KNOW. I kept looking around wondering, *'Where are all the men who need to hear this? Do they not see a problem? Or do they just not care?'*"

SINGING A NEW SONG

At this moment, I was being invited to join the choir. My line was supposed to be, "I KNOW!" But it suddenly felt wrong. My synapses were firing in a different direction. I said instead, "Megan, your company recently sponsored a conference for African Americans in your industry. Did you go to it?"

"Well… no." The gears began to click into place in her mind. "I didn't attend the one for Asian-Americans either. Nor the one for Latinx and Hispanic industry professionals."

We were back on the same page. I admitted, "I didn't either. But I'm guessing they each focused on all the ways their constituents are being discouraged, frustrated, and undervalued at work. I bet there were a lot of statistics about pay inequality and benefit plans that don't meet their needs. Everyone in the room had probably already lived that data in real time. At some point, one of them whispered to a friend, *'Where are all the white people who need to hear this? Do they not see a problem, or do they not care?'*

"You and I aren't seeing their struggles because they're not daily realities *for us*. Men don't see ours for the same reason. Let's change that. We should go to the MLK breakfast and the Chinese New Year celebration and the Pride Parade. Let's invite men to go with us to the women's conferences. Let's stop focusing on our own problems and start being allies to others."

Megan agreed. "We need to be more curious and sit in the discomfort. We should admit what we don't know and listen with open hearts."

After our conversation, I began volunteering as a mentor within professional associations for under-represented groups (specifically: veterans, African-Americans, and Asian-Americans). At a large corporate event, I grabbed a microphone and invited 300 men to attend the next women's conference.

Megan has made similar changes and has since moved into the executive ranks within her company. She says she is now explicit about the importance of curiosity and openness as part of her leadership style.

We haven't changed the world yet, but we have changed ourselves. That seems like the right starting point. I truly believe that we can only ask for support to the extent that we are willing to be allies to others.

PART FIVE:
BEYOND DIVERSITY
TO INCLUSION

"Diversity is being invited to the party; inclusion is being asked to dance."
– Verna Myers

"Be kind whenever possible. It is always possible."
– Dalai Lama

CHAPTER 27.
COVERING

Diversity is not just about demographics. Our experiences, work styles, and other factors all play important roles in our group interactions. The more perspectives you have in your network, the more likely you are to notice when you're having or witnessing a "round-headed conversation" (see Chapter 6).

How might your conversations at work be different, or how might you adjust your wording, if you knew that your boss grew up in foster care, had a spouse with an addiction problem, or had a child with a mental illness or physical disability? What are the odds that he or she has a family member with a criminal record or lost a close friend to suicide?

In any one year in the United States,

- 18.5 percent of adults are living with a diagnosed mental illness[86]
- 19 percent of adults have a permanent or temporary disability[87]
- 19 percent have been the victim of a recent crime[88]

In our lifetimes as Americans,

- 14 percent of us will experience homelessness[89]

- 5 percent will have been imprisoned, although this statistic is much higher (29 percent) for the subset of Americans who are also black and male[90]
- 10 percent will struggle with addiction to drugs or alcohol[91]
- 5 percent will survive cancer[92]

YOU CAN'T ALWAYS SEE DIVERSITY...

The conversations we have, and the things we say when we think we're in a room full of "round-headed people like us" can be extremely damaging to our working relationships. I once had a colleague who had left an emotionally and physically abusive marriage. We worked in retail, and one of the [male] stock managers announced that we were out of "wife-beaters," using a particularly callous term for sleeveless, white undershirts. My coworker felt as if her recent trauma was being trivialized, that her experience was the subject of ridicule. It takes an ally to make a space for the person who has been victimized. A situation like this requires a "round-headed" ally to step in and say, "That was inappropriate..."

...BECAUSE PEOPLE HIDE THEIR DIFFERENCES

Many people are familiar with the phrase *in the closet*, which typically describes LGBTQ people who keep their sexual orientation or gender identity a secret. An estimated 53 percent of the LGBTQ population are not out at work.[93] This is no surprise considering that a majority of states lack employment protections for LGBTQ workers.[94]

Still, the closet is not the exclusive domain of the LGBTQ community. People hide their invisible differences in many ways. What's more, even when a difference is visible or known, individuals engage in *covering* behavior to downplay certain aspects of a stigmatized identity.

---

covering, *verb*, to downplay a trait that is associated with a stigmatized identity

---

The term *covering* was first used in 1963 by American sociologist Erving Goffman[95]. Kenji Yoshino elaborated on this concept in his 2006 book *Covering:The Hidden Assault on Our Civil Rights.*[96]

By trying to protect ourselves from overt discrimination, we open ourselves to the countless indignities of being invisible. Rather than confront stereotypes, we internalize guilt and shame. The result of all of this "hiding in plain sight" is that we are less productive, less effective, and less connected to one another. In the next two chapters, we'll discuss why this is and how we can overcome it.

CHAPTER 28.
MICROAGGRESSIONS:
YOU *SHOULD* SWEAT THE
SMALL STUFF

Imagine for a moment that every time you interacted with one of your coworkers (we'll call them Pat), you walked away with a papercut. Every handshake, every meeting, every email or phone call results in a papercut, right in that webbing between your fingers.

The first time it happens, you may not make the connection. The second time, you may assume that it was an accident or a coincidence. The third time, you decide to speak up. Pat says you're being too sensitive. "Maybe," Pat says, "it's your fault you're getting papercuts in painful places." The trend continues, ad nauseum.

At what point would you begin to avoid Pat? When would you start to limit your interactions to "only when absolutely necessary"? How long would it be before you decide that it is never, ever absolutely necessary?

If this colleague had an open position on their team, would you apply? Even if it were a promotion or your dream job? Would you encourage your friends to apply?

Probably not.

If Pat were your boss, would you file a formal complaint? Or would you feel silly because it's "just" a papercut?

INTERPERSONAL PAPERCUTS

Many people work with someone like "Papercut Pat." Except, for them, the problem comes in the form of Pat's verbal jabs, rolling eyes, derisive comments, insensitive nicknames, harmful assumptions, intrusive questions, or similar behaviors. Many people *are* someone's Papercut Pat, and don't even know it!

These behaviors, called *microaggressions*, are like emotional papercuts that we inflict upon one another, often without realizing it. We say things or make assumptions that are rooted in ignorance or obliviousness, if not outright hostility. But these seemingly small indignities have a big impact over time. I'm sure you've heard the phrase *"death by a thousand cuts."*

---

microaggression, *noun*, a comment or action that subtly and often unconsciously or unintentionally expresses a prejudiced attitude toward a member of a marginalized group (such as a racial minority)[97]

Microaggressions can impact your career in negative ways, whether you're the one inflicting them or the one wincing in emotional pain.

EXAMPLES

These behaviors come in many forms, and, again, may not be intentional. But just like Pat's papercuts, they take a toll.

- Asking a female colleague, "Who watches your kids when you travel for work?"
- Telling a black person that they are "so articulate"
- Asking an Asian-American where they're "really" from
- Asking trans people questions about their genitals
- Using derogatory terms to describe people who have physical or intellectual disabilities
- Asking older workers when they plan to retire

DO YOU WORK WITH "PAPERCUT PAT"?

When people make honest mistakes because they *just don't realize* they're being disrespectful, give them the benefit of the doubt. Use structured, constructive feedback to explain the impact of their behavior so they don't repeat the mistake. This is a great opportunity for allies to step in and educate others in a compassionate way. We shouldn't leave it to someone who has been hurt to fend for themselves, even when the injury is accidental.

On the other hand, if Pat's behavior is intentional or persistent, you may need to escalate your complaints to your manager, Pat's supervisor, or your Human Resources Department. If you are in a safe place, I encourage you to stand up to workplace bullies, **especially** when you see them abusing someone else. Let's all stick together and be strong for one another!

Here are some things you can say:

- "What you said was disrespectful. I hope you don't really feel that way."
- "You owe everyone here an apology for making them feel uncomfortable / devalued."
- "I have a tremendous amount of respect for [name of colleague], and I will not let you talk to/about them that way."
- "Your behavior is unacceptable. If you refuse to show everyone the professional respect we deserve, then we will go on without you."

An even better course of action is to prevent microaggressions in the first place. True leaders eliminate these behaviors by proactively placing themselves between abuser and victim before any damage can be done. How? By being authentic and transparent, and by making *themselves* vulnerable.

CHAPTER 29.
TELLING YOUR OWN STORIES

Transparency, authenticity, and vulnerability are tools anyone can use to create stronger relationships. For leaders who seek to be more inclusive, authentic storytelling can accelerate trust and shape culture within your organization.[98]

> **Authentic storytelling accelerates trust and shapes culture in organizations.**
>
> **#NetworkBeyondBias**

Transparency is the willingness to show that which we normally keep hidden. It derives from an attitude of servant leadership. For many leaders, a polished corporate persona may have gotten them to the top. Inclusive leaders, though, know that to cultivate talent broadly, they must drop the façade and connect on a human level. Transparency, then, is all about showing the person behind the fancy title.

transparent, *adjective*, free from pretense or deceit; characterized by visibility or accessibility of information especially concerning business practices[99]

Authenticity, the ability to present oneself with integrity, demands high levels of both self-awareness and compassion. In being authentic, leaders align their stories, personae, and relationships

173

with their core values. People tend to describe authentic leaders with words like *relatable, down-to-earth,* or *accessible.* Authentic leaders haven't lost touch with the journey that led them to their destination.

authentic, *adjective,* true to one's own personality, spirit, or character[100]

Finally, vulnerability requires incredible courage and self-confidence. To be vulnerable means to show our weaknesses. Vulnerable leaders share the lessons they learned from failures and mistakes. They tell the stories of times when they weren't heroes and needed someone else to save the day. Vulnerable leaders admit they don't have all the answers, all the time. Exposing one's own flaws, blind spots, and development opportunities is scary stuff. But, as I've already mentioned, this is the work of leaders!

vulnerable, *adjective,* open to attack or damage[101]

Regardless of your tenure or title, you can lead others by example. If you want to connect with and inspire others, you must be both brave and humble. These are the hallmarks of true leadership.

Here are some prompts to help you get started.

YOUR VALUES

Share a story from your childhood, teenage years, or early adulthood that was a defining moment for you. What brought you to the crossroads? What core values drove your decision? What did you learn about yourself? When was the last time you told yourself or someone else this story and why?

YOUR JOURNEY

If you are in a position of power, such as a corporate leader, think back to when you were just starting your climb up the organizational ladder. Was there a time when you struggled to be heard or taken seriously? How did that feel? What steps did you take to cope with your environment or to change your approach? If you were in that situation today, how might you handle it differently?

YOUR STRUGGLES

Talk about times you have struggled – financially, academically, professionally, or personally. Who helped you? What mistakes did you make? What did you learn? Do you now view this struggle as a source of pride?

Was there ever a time you didn't fit in? How did that feel? How has this experience influenced your leadership style?

In what aspects of your job or life do you struggle? When do you ask for help? Are there times when you refuse to seek help because you don't want to appear weak, incompetent, or vulnerable?

YOUR MISTAKES

Think about a time when you missed a chance to live up to your values. What was the situation? Why do you now feel you made the wrong decision? What options did you have, and what drove your choice? What lesson did you learn?

Talk about a time when your beliefs about something or someone were inaccurate or incomplete. How did you become aware of your error? What work did you have to do – internally or externally – to bridge the gap? How might the situation have unfolded if you hadn't changed your mind? Did you ultimately learn more about yourself?

Visit the website for story examples and printable worksheets to help you craft your own leadership stories.

WWW.NETWORKBEYONDBIAS.COM

STORYTELLING MATTERS

We all need role models. When those role models have flaws or limitations we can relate to, we become even more invested in their success. The people who look up to you want to be able to see themselves in you. They want to feel connected to you and your story. When you engage in authentic storytelling, you provide that vital connection.

CHAPTER 30.
SAYING
"YOU'RE WELCOME"

Identifying missing perspectives in your network is relatively easy. Finding people who can fill those gaps isn't terribly difficult. But how do you attract people who differ from you? How do you make yourself the light in the room to which they are drawn? This chapter introduces three pillars of inclusive networking that you can use, not just to bring people to you, but also to bring out the best in them.

ACCEPTANCE

The first step in inclusive networking is acceptance. In fact, you cannot be inclusive of someone at all until you can accept them as they are.

accept, verb, to endure without protest or reaction[102]

For many of us, our first instinct when we encounter conflict is to attempt to convert or persuade the other party to our way of thinking. Instead, go into the conversation with the mindset that the person you are about to meet is an expert.

In *The 7 Habits of Highly Effective People,* Stephen Covey advises us, "Seek first to understand, then to be understood."[103] For many of us, though, either critical thinking or pre-conceived notions become obstacles to understanding. Asking challenging questions can be perceived as disagreement, resulting in more conflict and greater barriers to understanding. That's why I try to accept first.

It was this critical step that led me to be a vocal, if imperfect, ally to the transgender community (see Chapter 21). I had spent so much time getting in my own way, trying to understand the "why," that I missed the whole point. Eventually, I realized I don't need to know why something exists to acknowledge that it's there. Similarly, I don't need to understand how someone developed their worldview to accept that it exists. So why would I require a complete understanding of the social context and psychological frameworks that led to someone else's identity, just to believe that their identity is real?

When you meet someone new, accept them for who they are. Accept that their experiences, opinions, and talents are theirs and theirs alone. Once you've mastered accepting what is, you'll be amazed at how much more quickly you can move to understanding.

RESPECT

Respect is the next essential tool for inclusive behaviors. My favorite definition of *respect* comes from my kids' karate dojo:

respect, *verb*, to feel or show polite or courteous responses to the wishes or judgments of others

You'll notice that there is no mention of agreement. No requirement exists to give the person money for their cause. On the other hand, there's no room there for hostility. You can disagree, just be polite about it. That's it. Easy peasy. Right?

Let's work with some concrete examples to make it real.

- You probably know how to spell and pronounce your CEO's first and last name.
- Imagine an executive at your company expressed a strong political view after hours. She asks for your opinion, which is in contrast to hers. You would likely find a diplomatic response, and you would do so quickly.
- When your boss presents during a meeting, you don't roll your eyes, scroll through Facebook, or interrupt her. (At least, I hope you don't.)
- You're aware that your most important client is allergic to shellfish, so you avoid taking him to seafood restaurants when you pay him a visit.

You're probably polite and considerate when someone outranks you. But can you say that about yourself in other interactions? Watch your behaviors for a few weeks and see if you treat everyone with genuine respect. If not, you're going to limit your ability to engage in inclusive networking. Do some deep reflection on your biases, assumptions, and intentions. Then think about the impact you might be having on the people around you.

EMPATHY

The ultimate tool for inclusive networking is empathy. Once you've mastered acceptance and started practicing universal respect, it's time to level up.

Empathy is the ability to understand how someone else is feeling, and then to adapt your own behavior accordingly. If you're thinking, "WHOA. That's awfully touchy-feely," you may be right. But that doesn't make it unimportant. In fact, it's an easy way to set yourself apart as a great leader in a hypermasculine or otherwise toxic work environment.

---

empathy, *noun*, the action of understanding, being aware of, being sensitive to, and vicariously experiencing the feelings, thoughts, and experience of another of either the past or present without having the feelings, thoughts, and experience fully communicated in an objectively explicit manner; also : the capacity for this

---

Perhaps you think having empathy is like having a sixth sense. The truth is, empathy is a skill that can be developed over time. Start small, by naming your own feelings as you have them. Over time, build up the courage to ask others how they're feeling. For example, you might say, "I heard your presentation went really well this morning. That must make you feel proud of your work." It feels weird at first, but the feedback you'll get (watch for verbal and nonverbal cues) will make you want to continue. Pretty soon, people will be coming to you for advice because you're so good at understanding them! When this happens, you'll know your inclusive networking efforts are truly paying off: you've become a mentor!

> **Empathy is a skill that can be developed over time. #NetworkBeyondBias**

If you want to dive into this topic further, I highly recommend *Emotional Intelligence 2.0* by Travis Bradberry and Jean Greaves.[104] The book includes a self-assessment to help you target your efforts where you need the most help.

CHAPTER 31.
YOU ARE RESPONSIBLE FOR YOUR IMPACT

Remember from Chapter 1, our identity is at the heart of everything we do, think, and experience. When our negative impacts don't match our good intentions, we suffer a crisis of identity. The natural response is to get defensive and explain why you're a "good person" and the other person is wrong. Instead, try to learn from your mistakes with humility and an open heart.

SEVEN QUESTIONS FOR SELF-REFLECTION

Think there's no way you're an office bully? Ask yourself the following questions, answering each one honestly:

1. In the last six months, have I told someone they're being "too sensitive" in response to something I said? Have I told anyone I work with that they "can't take a joke"?
2. Can I remember the last time I made a joke that targeted someone's gender or gender identity, race, ethnicity, sexual orientation, or disability?
3. Have I recently made a generalization, realized I was in "mixed company," and said, "Oh, I didn't mean *you*"?

4. Has anyone asked me to stop making certain types of comments or called me a bully? Do people roll their eyes in exasperation?

5. Do I feel defensive when someone points out my behavior?

6. Do I feel like I am better / smarter / more competent than others and therefore have a *right* to denigrate them?

7. Do I regularly exclude certain people from discussions so I won't have to watch what I say?

HOW TO STOP BEING AN OFFICE BULLY

Do some soul searching. If you're lashing out at others, perhaps it's because you feel threatened or insecure. Work on being vulnerable, on not having all the answers, and on lifting others up for their experience and expertise.

---

bully, *noun*, a blustering, browbeating person; *especially* : one who is habitually cruel, insulting, or threatening to others who are weaker, smaller, or in some way vulnerable

---

Make public and private apologies. If you have belittled, ignored, or intimidated others, apologize to them privately. Next, apologize publicly to the people who witnessed your behavior. You not only made those witnesses feel uncomfortable, you also made them complicit if they were afraid to stand up to you.

Ask someone you trust to watch your behavior and call you out on it if it continues. Practice receiving constructive feedback gracefully. Ask for time to think about the feedback, even if you disagree with it.

Admitting that you've been disrespectful in the past is difficult, but your reputation and relationships are worth it.

#NetworkBeyondBias

RECOVERING FROM HONEST MISTAKES

We all make mistakes when interacting with other people, especially when their values, perspectives, or identities differ markedly from our own. Despite our best intentions, we may ask an intrusive question, choose our words poorly, or hurt someone's feelings. Remember, while we will judge ourselves on our intent, others are likely to judge us based on our impact. Two questions become important: (1) How do I know if I've hurt someone? and (2) How do I set things right?

Assessing the Damage

When people are uncomfortable, they usually show it. If someone looks around for support or gets suddenly quiet, you may have crossed a line. Many times when we see that we've hurt someone, we try to push through so we can ignore the damage we've done. We assume that if we don't acknowledge them, our transgressions will be forgotten, or at least forgiven.

In some cases, we may miss the moment entirely. If we are solely focused on our own needs or objectives, we may not notice the nonverbal cues of our colleagues. Spend some time reflecting on your interactions. Were you supportive of and engaged in your coworkers' interests, or were you preoccupied with your own agenda?

Making Amends

To build trusting relationships, we must hold ourselves accountable to being worthy of that trust. If you catch yourself in the moment, address the situation immediately. Show vulnerability by admitting your mistake and expressing a sincere desire to be more inclusive. If you're embarrassed, say so.

When you realize you've made a mistake after the fact, make a conscious effort to Put Yourself on Notice (see Chapter 3). After you've spent some time with your finger on your Pause Button, share what you've learned about yourself with others involved.

Even the most well-intentioned people make mistakes. When you're in a new situation, or in a working relationship with someone new, mistakes are inevitable. Learn from your mistakes, grow, and avoid making them again.

My Own Embarrassing Mistake

When I first met a coworker, Tammy, she indicated her spouse had cancer. I sent a card telling her how glad I was to meet her and how I hoped her husband's radiation treatments were going well. A few days later, she thanked me for the card.

Weeks passed, and I was having lunch with someone who had worked with Tammy for years. I asked him how Tammy's husband was doing. He said, "You mean her *wife*." I was stunned. As a bisexual woman, I know how hard it is to be constantly aware of the pronouns one uses to describe one's partner. I actively listen for people who are "playing the pronoun game" so I can step up as a vocal ally. I was *sure* I'd heard Tammy refer to her husband. But, of course, she had not used that word.

My reaction quickly changed from stunned to mortified. Here I was, daily advocating for the inclusion of LGBTQ perspectives at work, and I had marginalized a new coworker because I wasn't listening. The same day, I called Tammy to apologize for my ignorance and insensitivity. She was gracious and forgiving. Sadly, Tammy's wife passed a short while later, and Tammy has since retired. Life can be so cruel. People, on the other hand, needn't be.

CHAPTER 32.
HOW DIVERSE IS YOUR NETWORK?

"Everyone thinks of changing the world, but no one thinks of changing himself."
– Leo Tolstoy

In this chapter, we will assess the depth and breadth of your CHAMP Network, one step at a time. You can only manage that which you can measure, and you can only see progress if you have a definite starting point. Think of this as the first step of the journey that awaits you!

You'll use the following grid for your assessment. You can write in this book, create your own version on a notepad, or download a printable version at NetworkBeyondBias.com. Each column represents a step in the assessment process. You'll complete the columns in order, top to bottom, starting with the "CHAMP" column on the left.

> Visit the website for a printable assessment grid and a video tutorial.
>
> **WWW.NETWORKBEYONDBIAS.COM**

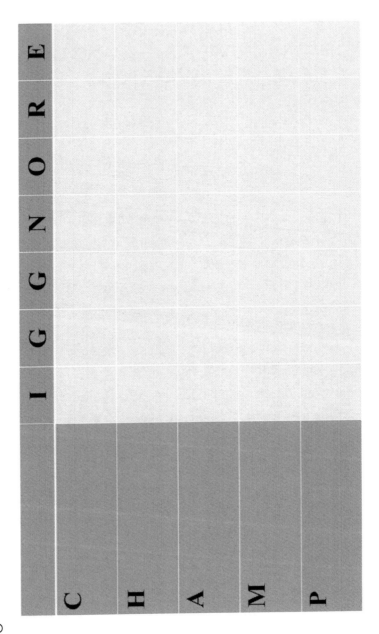

STEP 1: WHO ARE YOUR CHAMPs?

First, we'll assess the depth of your professional network. The goal is to determine how many critical relationships you are cultivating … and which ones may be missing. By the end of Step 1, you'll have up to five names that will bring your CHAMP network to life. Let's get started!

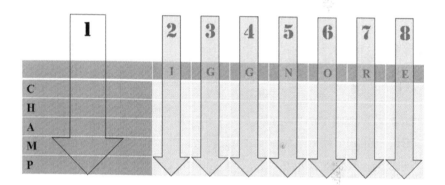

C is for Customer

Think of the Customer (see Chapter 12) with whom you've most recently interacted or with whom you have the best relationship. This is the person you tend to call when you need a Customer's perspective. Put their name in the "C" line of Column 1. *If you haven't talked to a Customer in the last three months, leave this spot blank.* If you have met with multiple Customers, list only one for this exercise.

H is for Hire

Quickly review Chapter 13. Whom did you most recently hire? Is there someone you helped get a job, introduced to a recruiter, or referred as a freelancer? Have you recently written a letter of recommendation for someone you know? Warm introductions (like those in Chapter 10) count; endorsing someone's skills on LinkedIn does not. Put the person's name on the "H" line of Column 1. Again, if you haven't attempted to help someone land a job, gig, or promotion in the last three months, leave this spot blank.

A is for Associate

Which of your peers do you call when you're having a bad day or need feedback on an idea? Which of your teammates did you most recently invite to lunch? Review the description of Associates in Chapter 14. Add your Associate's name to the "A" line in Column 1. If you don't have a peer confidante at work, or if you haven't connected with them recently, leave this cell blank.

M is for Mentor

If you have a formal Mentor (*see* Chapter 15), list them in the "M" line of Column 1. If not, is there someone whose advice you frequently seek? Tell that person you think of them as a Mentor, and then put their name in the grid. Leave this line blank if you don't have someone who meets these criteria or if you haven't spoken with them in the last few months.

P is for Protégé

Finally, who in your network are you helping to build up and pull forward in their career? Are you serving as a formal mentor in your company, community, or professional associations? You know how this works: put their name in the "P" line of Column 1, if you have someone to name. If not, re-read Chapter 16 to remind yourself why this is so important!

How many people were you able to list? If fewer than five, your first job is to fill this network...*but not yet!*

STEPS 2 – 7: WHAT PERSPECTIVES DOES YOUR NETWORK IGGNORE?

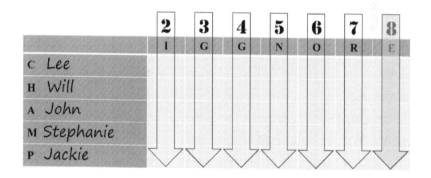

		2	3	4	5	6	7	8
		I	G	G	N	O	R	E
c	Lee							
H	Will							
A	John							
M	Stephanie							
P	Jackie							

At this point, the first column of your grid should look a little like the one above. Don't worry if you don't have a name in each row.

Remember, this is only the beginning! Next, we'll assess the breadth of your network.

Step 2: Industry

What is your primary industry? If your role or company spans multiple industries, choose the one industry about which you consider yourself most knowledgeable. Now, put an X in Column 2 for each CHAMP who falls outside your primary industry.

Often when I do this exercise with a live audience, people will tell me their list not only excludes other industries, but is limited to their own company. To make matters worse, sometimes all their CHAMPS come from their own department!

Why are close-proximity CHAMP networks so problematic? In a corporate restructure, large departments or entire divisions may be eliminated with the stroke of a pen. Smaller companies may be acquired by larger firms, change direction to seize new opportunities, or dissolve entirely. Who will you call for a job tomorrow if your five closest connections have lost their jobs on the same day? How will you connect your coworkers to recruiters or hiring managers (to grow your Hire Network) if you don't know anyone outside your company? And how will you have the energy to do so if you're stressed about whether you can find another job?

Step 3: Generation

The first G in the top row stands for Generation. You may not know the exact ages of the people around you, or you may be unfamiliar with where the generations begin and end. That's okay. For this exercise, put an X in Column 3 for each CHAMP you believe is at least ten years older or younger than you.

Many people have mentors that are at least ten years their senior and protégés who are much younger than themselves. Consider for a moment what you might gain from being mentored by someone from a younger generation. Furthermore, what skills or experience might you be able to offer peers who are significantly older than you? Think beyond obvious relationship patterns, and you could make some astounding connections!

Step 4: Gender / Gender Identity

In Column 4, place an X next to each of your CHAMPs whose gender or gender identity (see Chapter 21) differs from your own. Cisgender women tend to struggle to find mentors and receive effective feedback. Trans women and nonbinary individuals are often excluded from the workforce entirely because they lack sponsors, support, or even access to restrooms. Trans men, on the other hand, may be able to "pass" at work but face tremendous levels of stress over the fear of being outed. How are you positioning yourself and your CHAMP network to bridge these gaps?

Step 5: National Origin / Native Language

If any of your CHAMPs came from a different country or speak a different native language than you, place an X next to their name in Column 5. As noted in Chapter 2, it is difficult for us to see the culture around us because it is everywhere. When we build relationships with people from other countries and cultures, we start to understand what we take for granted about the world. I also recommend that people expose themselves to as many different accents and languages as possible. With greater exposure comes less friction in communication across dialects and distance.

Step 6: Sexual Orientation

Column 6 is where you'll mark if your CHAMPS are of a different sexual orientation than you. I don't recommend you survey your coworkers about their sexual orientation. In fact, I'd strongly advise against doing so. However, if you ask about people's families, you are likely to learn a lot about them. On the other hand, if you never ask someone about their weekend, their spouse, or other friendly questions, you're not going to build long-term, trusting relationships.

Listen to the pronouns people use. Are they "playing the pronoun game"? If so, be respectful, and understand that they may feel uncomfortable or threatened. Ask yourself how you can create a safer, more welcoming environment for others.

Step 7: Race and Ethnicity

How racially and ethnically diverse is your CHAMP Network? Mark all the people outside your own racial identity or ethnic background in Column 7. If your network lacks *visible* diversity (see Chapter 23), people from different backgrounds are unlikely to seek you out, trust you, or consider you as an ally. If you are a member of a visible minority group, you'll need relationships with people "on the inside" to help you move ahead.

STEP 8: HOW DEEP ARE YOUR RELATIONSHIPS?

In Step 1, we looked at the depth of your *network*. In Steps 2 through 7, you assessed your network's breadth. In this final step, we'll consider the depth of your individual *relationships.*

	I	G	G	N	O	R	E
c Lee	X		X		X		
H Will	X	X	X		X	X	
A John		X	X		X		
M Stephanie	X	X			X	X	
P Jackie		X	X	X	X	X	

The "E" in Column 8 stands for Exchange. Recall the stories you crafted (in Chapter 29) that make you a transparent, authentic, and vulnerable leader. For each person in your CHAMP network, consider whether you've exchanged personal stories about defining moments in your lives. Do you know the values, challenges, and worldviews that make your CHAMPs who they are? Have you shared yours with them? If so, put an X next to each CHAMP contact that has gotten to this level of depth and connection. What have you gained from building stronger relationships with these individuals? How much trust have you left on the table with the others?

YOUR COMPLETED ASSESSMENT

Your completed assessment should look something like the one below. You may have empty rows or columns or you may have lots of cells filled. Regardless, you may be very satisfied with your results, and you may also feel that you have significant work to do.

	I	G	G	N	O	R	E
c Lee	X		X		X		X
H Will	X	X	X		X	X	
A John		X	X		X		X
M Stephanie	X	X			X	X	X
P Jackie		X	X	X	X	X	

The completed grid, above, is my own network assessment at the time of this writing. Were I to sketch it out again while you're reading this, it would look a little bit different. Some of the names change almost daily. I stay engaged with my Customer Network, and I am constantly connecting people in my Hire Network to managers, recruiters, freelancers, and business partners. I have multiple Protégés with whom I meet regularly; Jackie happened to call me this week for some advice.

The first time I took my own assessment, though, I had blank rows and empty columns. Seeing these missed opportunities on paper spurred me into action, and I changed my networking behaviors accordingly. I've since built a larger professional network, adding more diversity *on purpose*. You, too, can use the tools in this book to improve the depth and breadth of your network and relationships very quickly.

Snap a photo of your completed grid and post it to social media!

#NetworkBeyondBias

WHERE TO GO FROM HERE

Fill Your CHAMP Network

If there are blank rows in your grid, make a plan to fill the missing perspectives. Review Chapters 11 through 16 to remind yourself why these relationships are important to cultivate and maintain. Set priorities based on your current career goals. Use the tips in Chapters 7 through 10 to start making connections.

Be Intentional About Diversity

Does your grid have empty columns? Remember, diversity doesn't happen by accident. Our natural tendency is to surround ourselves with people who are as similar to us as possible (see Chapters 5 and 6). Think about what perspectives your network is missing, and intentionally seek out people who can complement your worldview. Ensure that you are being inclusive and welcoming along the way (revisit Chapters 29 through 32).

Come Out, Come Out, Whoever You Are

A full column in your grid may indicate that you are a member of an underrepresented group. If so, spend some time thinking about ways your perspective may need to be amplified within your network. Are you engaging in covering behaviors like those discussed in Chapter 28? How could people in your network benefit from learning more about your point of view? How could you drive innovation or understanding by telling your own stories? What might those contributions mean for your career?

Don't Leave Trust on the Table

If you have a broad and diverse network that stretches across your industry and beyond, consider the strength of your individual relationships. Use the storytelling tips in Chapter 30 to connect with people on a deeper level. These trusting relationships are the ones that last beyond our tenure with a company or the fulfillment of a contract. Make sure you are networking for the long term.

Go Beyond the Grid

You've probably noticed that many important dimensions of diversity are missing from this assessment tool. There's no column for different educational backgrounds, levels of physical ability, religious affiliation, or neurodiversity, for example. I've used the last column as a catch-all for many of these types of differences. You may think that's lazy, and you may be right. My goal is to *get you thinking about your network differently*. If you're finding glaring omissions in my approach, then I've achieved my goal! By all means, stretch this grid out with as many columns and dimensions as you wish. The point, after all, is to expand your network as broadly and deeply as possible, including as many different people as you can!

 Build trusting relationships to ensure you are networking for the long term.
#NetworkBeyondBias

Chapter 33.
Why Executives (Almost) All Look Alike

If executives want to see more diversity among their ranks, they need to stop promoting only those employees who are reflections of themselves. What's more, tomorrow's leaders must start diversifying their networks *now* to change the view at the top for coming generations. While no one person bears the responsibility for executive demographics, we each have a responsibility to understand our role in perpetuating them.

- White women hold 23 CEO spots in the S&P 500 at the time of this writing.[105] The record of 28 women was set in 2017. At our most gender diverse, 47 percent of the labor force overall[106] comprised only 5.6 percent of the people in charge. This is despite women having more education, on average, than men.[107]
- Three black men currently run Fortune 500 companies.[108] There have only been fifteen in history.[109] At the time of this writing, there are **no black women** in Fortune 500 (or S&P 500) CEO roles.[110]
- Executive representation is even worse for Latinx workers, Native Americans, Hawaiians and Pacific Islanders.
- Among the Fortune 500, the list of openly LGBTQ CEOs includes Tim Cook of Apple, and that's it. End of list.

While it's true that each company can have only one CEO, the diversity of the next leadership tier is similarly lacking. In fact, the higher you rise in a company's ranks, the less diversity you will see. Some of this is certainly the result of institutionalized, systemic barriers to under-represented groups. But I believe it is equally the result of personal proximity and the affinity bias inherent in individuals' professional networks.

Tomorrow's leaders must start diversifying their professional networks now. #NetworkBeyondBias

If your current executive team assessed their CHAMP network (as you did in Chapter 32), how rich and full would their grids look? How different would their results be today, compared to what they would have been ten, fifteen, or twenty years ago? My guess is that there would not be many marks in Columns 2 through 7, then or now.

Despite some small gains in executive representation, we cannot take the inevitability of progress for granted. As recently as 2017, Deloitte announced that it would eliminate ERGs in favor of other diversity and inclusion initiatives. As part of the announcement, one Deloitte executive said he didn't know "if [he] even had a role" to play in the company's ERGs. I hope executives elsewhere recognize that this is how *a majority of employees feel about their companies' leadership teams!*

Furthermore, leaders at all levels owe it to ourselves and our followers to sit somewhere we don't feel like we belong. Everyone can benefit from the experience of being "other," at least occasionally. What does it say to your employees if you are unwilling to experience briefly what they live daily? What does it say about your willingness to be transparent, authentic, and vulnerable if you cannot be troubled to leave your corner office?

WHAT YOU CAN DO RIGHT NOW

If diversity and inclusion are important to you, speak up. Your voice and example may be the one that makes a difference, if not for the entire company, then maybe for one person who was feeling like they didn't belong.

Here are my suggestions for having an impact, whatever your relationship to a company.

Executives

Work with your senior leadership teams to quantify the value of your company's diversity initiatives. Consider adding ever more perspectives to your corporate conversations. Carefully consider the internal and external messaging that comes with any changes to your diversity strategies.

Tell stories that champion people from diverse backgrounds and demographics. Advocate for making self-identification an option for employees from underrepresented groups. Track the retention, promotion, and job satisfaction of those employees over time. Fill your talent and succession pipelines with intentional diversity.

Personally promote and attend ERG activities within your company. Conduct listening tours within your company that include ERG representatives.

Ensure supplier diversity by seeking vendors with Minority Business Enterprise (MBE), Women's Business Enterprise (WBE), and LGBT Business Enterprise (LGBTBE) designations.

Employees

Build your network with intentional diversity. Refer job candidates from diverse backgrounds. Connect people who may not otherwise move in the same circles.

Join an ERG if you haven't already. Try to start one if your employer doesn't offer them. Talk to your manager, executives, and others in your company about the impact ERGs have (or could have), from your perspective.

If you are a member of an affinity group ERG (one that's "for you"), invite an ally or potential ally to join you. Ask a colleague how you can get involved in an ERG that's outside your affinity group.

Speak up, whenever you can, wherever you can, about who you are and why it matters. Be the role model you needed five, ten, or thirty years ago.

Listen to others' stories and learn how to be an effective ally from their perspectives. Go to the conference that's not for you.

Everyone Else

Customers, stockholders, college students, and potential job candidates can also pressure companies to be more inclusive. Talk about the importance of diversity during job interviews, sales presentations, trade shows, shareholder meetings, user group forums, and any other opportunity you have. Ask salespeople and recruiters about their company's diversity initiatives.

Don't underestimate your influence. Companies care what their external stakeholders think.

MY INVITATION TO YOU

I started Lead at Any Level, LLC to help busy professionals build skills in leadership, diversity and inclusion, and career management. My presentations, training sessions, and coaching programs include original insights and content you won't find anywhere else. I want to help companies find and develop their "hidden" leaders, transform their workforce demographics, and accelerate organic growth through well-connected, emotionally intelligent employees. Together, we can set the stage for tomorrow's leaders to be more inclusive, and we can start right now!

Are you on a mission? Do our interests and goals overlap? Let's get acquainted and learn how we can help each other!

- http://www.NetworkBeyondBias.com
- http://LinkedIn.com/in/AmyCWaninger
- On Twitter at @AmyCWaninger and @LeadAtAnyLevel

We have so much work to do. Use your gifts to their fullest. Help others do the same. All hands on deck!

ACKNOWLEDGMENTS

My husband, Scott, has been an amazing partner throughout this process. I love you, and I appreciate the sacrifices you make so I can chase my ambitions. To my beautiful, bright, and compassionate children: Brandon, Nick, and Vivian, thank you for your patience and support.

I am grateful for the guidance and encouragement of my own CHAMP Network: the incomparable and inspiring Jennifer Brown; Cathy Fyock, the Business Book Strategist; my expanded editorial team of Natalie Siston, Scott Waninger, Sabrina Bristo, John Leonard, and Vera Emmons; Tony Cañas, Carly Burnham, and the rest of the InsNerds crew; the CPCU Society Diversity Committee; my fellow Toastmasters; my Twitter tribe; all the individuals who provided early reviews of the book; and, finally, everyone whose stories and perspectives informed both these pages and my own professional growth.

APPENDICES

GLOSSARY

accept, *verb*, to endure without protest or reaction

affinity bias, *noun*, the tendency to surround ourselves with people we believe are similar to us in some way

ally, *verb*, side with or support

amygdala, *noun*, an almond -shaped mass of gray matter in the front part of the temporal lobe of the cerebrum that is part of the limbic system and is involved in the processing and expression of emotions, especially anger and fear

assigned gender, *noun*, the gender initially proclaimed at an individual's birth (typically male, female, or intersex)

associate, *noun*, peer

authentic, *adjective*, true to one's own personality, spirit, or character

bias, *noun*, a particular tendency, trend, inclination, feeling, or opinion, especially one that is preconceived or unreasoned

bully, *noun*, a blustering, browbeating person; especially : one who is habitually cruel, insulting, or threatening to others who are weaker, smaller, or in some way vulnerable

cisgender, *adjective*, describes someone whose gender identity matches the gender they were assigned at birth. Avoid using the terms "normal," "real man," or "real woman" to describe cisgender people

cover, *verb*, to downplay a trait that is associated with a stigmatized identity

customer, *noun*, one that purchases a commodity or service (or one that has that potential to do so)

elevator pitch, *noun*, a succinct and persuasive sales pitch

empathy, *noun*, the action of understanding, being aware of, being sensitive to, and vicariously experiencing the feelings, thoughts, and experience of another of either the past or present without having the feelings, thoughts, and experience fully communicated in an objectively explicit manner; also : the capacity for this

Employee Resource Group (ERG), *noun*, voluntary, employee-led groups that foster a diverse, inclusive workplace aligned with organizational mission, values, goals, business practices, and objectives

gender confirmation, *noun*, a complicated and lengthy medical process whereby a person's physicality is altered to match their gender identity. Avoid using the term "sex change."

gender expression, *noun*, the way an individual presents their gender identity (typically masculine, feminine, or androgynous)

gender fluidity, *noun*, the notion that a person's gender identity or gender expression is not fixed

gender identity, *noun*, the gender with which an individual identifies (typically male, female, or nonbinary)

gender nonconforming, *adjective,* a catch-all term for gender-fluid and nonbinary individuals, and sometimes for individuals who choose a gender expression that violates societal norms

genderqueer, *adjective*, a term more often used by young, gender nonconforming people, and particularly people of color; this term carries an additional connotation of political activism. Avoid describing someone as "queer" (adjective) unless you know for sure an individual self-describes that way. Never use the word "queer" as a noun.

groupthink, *noun*, the lack of individual creativity, or a sense of personal responsibility, that is sometimes characteristic of group interaction

implicit association test, *noun*, a measure within social psychology designed to detect the strength of a person's automatic association between mental representations of objects (concepts) in memory

imposter syndrome, *noun*, as a collection of feelings of inadequacy that persist despite evident success

in-group, *noun*, a group of people sharing similar interests and attitudes, producing feelings of solidarity, community, and exclusivity.

Latinx, *adjective*, a person of Latin American origin or descent (used as a gender-neutral or non-binary alternative to Latino or Latina)

LGBTQ, *adjective*, Lesbian, Gay, Bisexual, Transgender, and Queer [Community]; variations include LGBT and LGBTQIA+

mentor, *noun*, a trusted counselor or guide

microaggression, *noun*, a comment or action that subtly and often unconsciously or unintentionally expresses a prejudiced attitude toward a member of a marginalized group (such as a racial minority)

network, *noun*, an association of individuals having a common interest, formed to provide mutual assistance, helpful information, or the like

network, *verb*, to cultivate professional relationships in a way that is mutually beneficial, creative, and expansive

neuroplasticity, *noun*, the capacity of the nervous system to develop new neuronal connections

personal brand, *noun*, the idea, conception, or mental image that others have about you

philtrum, *noun*, the vertical groove on the surface of the upper lip, below the septum of the nose; also: medial cleft, pause button

privilege, *noun*, (1) a right, immunity, or benefit enjoyed by a person beyond the advantages of most; (2) anything you don't have to worry about on a regular basis that is a routine source of frustration or anxiety for someone else

protégé, *noun*, one who is protected or trained or whose career is furthered by a person of experience, prominence, or influence

respect, *verb*, to feel or show polite or courteous responses to the wishes or judgments of others

self-image, *noun*, the idea, conception, or mental image one has of oneself

social identity, *noun*, a person's sense of who they are based on their group membership(s)

socialization, *noun*, a continuing process whereby an individual acquires a personal identity and learns the norms, values, behavior, and social skills appropriate to his or her social position

stereotype, *noun*, a widely held but fixed and oversimplified image or idea of a particular type of person or thing

transgender, or trans, *adjective*, describes someone whose gender identity differs from the gender they were assigned at birth. Avoid using the terms "transsexual" or "cross-dressing" to describe trans people.

transition, *noun*, the process of changing one's gender identity and/or gender expression, regardless of whether one undertakes the gender confirmation process. Avoid using the term "sex change."

transparent, *adjective*, free from pretense or deceit; characterized by visibility or accessibility of information especially concerning business practices

unconscious bias, *noun*, a preference that happens automatically, is outside of our control and is triggered by our brain making quick judgments and assessments of people and situations, influenced by our background, cultural environment and personal experiences

uptalk, *noun*, a manner of speaking in which declarative sentences are uttered with rising intonation at the end, as if they were questions.

values, *noun*, group conceptions of the relative desirability of things; deeply held convictions about what is important in life

vulnerable, *adjective*, open to attack or damage

INDEX

NOTES

Visit the website for a bibliography
with hyperlinks to cited sources

WWW.NETWORKBEYONDBIAS.COM

[1] Scanlon, Scott A. "What Diverse Candidates Look for From Employers." Hunt Scanlon Media. 2017. Accessed May 03, 2018. https://huntscanlon.com/diverse-candidates-look-employers/.

[2] Weissmann, Elena. "Female STEM Students Cite Isolation, Lack of Role Models." *Brown Daily Herald*. April 30, 2015. Accessed May 03, 2018. http://www.browndailyherald.com/2015/04/23/female-stem-students-cite-isolation-lack-of-role-models/.

[3] Rivera, Lauren A. "Guess Who Doesn't Fit In at Work." *The New York Times*. May 30, 2015. Accessed May 03, 2018. https://www.nytimes.com/2015/05/31/opinion/sunday/guess-who-doesnt-fit-in-at-work.html?_r=0.

[4] Rothwell, Jonathan. "Short on STEM Talent." U.S. News & World Report. September 15, 2014. Accessed May 03, 2018. https://www.usnews.com/opinion/articles/2014/09/15/the-stem-worker-shortage-is-real.

[5] PTI. "Retaining Human Talent a Concern Insurance Firms: Report." *The Financial Express*. June 01, 2017. Accessed May 03, 2018. https://www.financialexpress.com/industry/retaining-human-talent-a-concern-insurance-firms-report/696906/.

[6] Bidwell, Allie. "STEM Workforce No More Diverse Than 14 Years Ago." *U.S. News & World Report*. February 24, 2015. Accessed May 03, 2018. https://www.usnews.com/news/stem-solutions/articles/2015/02/24/stem-workforce-no-more-diverse-than-14-years-ago.

[7] Boyer, Sam. ""It Is All White Men over 40": Lack of Diversity among Insurance Execs." *Insurance Business.* June 08, 2017. Accessed May 03, 2018. https://www.insurancebusinessmag.com/us/news/breaking-news/it-is-all-white-men-over-40-lack-of-diversity-among-insurance-execs-69849.aspx#.WTnv19GvKBk.twitter.

[8] DiSalvo, David. "Your Brain Sees Even When You Don't." Forbes.com. June 22, 2013. Accessed May 29, 2018. https://www.forbes.com/sites/daviddisalvo/2013/06/22/your-brain-sees-even-when-you-dont/#3a7322f7116a

[9] "Amygdala." Dictionary.com. Accessed May 03, 2018. http://www.dictionary.com/browse/amygdala.

[10] "Bias." Dictionary.com. Accessed May 03, 2018. http://www.dictionary.com/browse/bias.

[11] Gann, Jen. "Babies As Young As 6 Months Old Show Racial Bias." The Cut. April 13, 2017. Accessed May 03, 2018. https://www.thecut.com/2017/04/babies-as-young-as-6-months-old-show-racial-bias.html.

[12] Slater, Alan, Charlotte Von Der Schulenburg, Elizabeth Brown, Marion Badenoch, George Butterworth, Sonia Parsons, and Curtis Samuels. "Newborn Infants Prefer Attractive Faces." *Egyptian Journal of Medical Human Genetics.* April 21, 2002. Accessed May 03, 2018. https://www.sciencedirect.com/science/article/pii/S016363839890011X.

[13] "Values, Basic Concepts of Sociology Guide." Sociology Guide. Accessed May 03, 2018. http://www.sociologyguide.com/basic-concepts/Values.php.

[14] "Socialization." Dictionary.com. Accessed May 03, 2018. http://www.dictionary.com/browse/socialization.

[15] McLeod, Saul. "Saul McLeod." Simply Psychology. January 01, 1970. Accessed May 03, 2018. https://www.simplypsychology.org/social-identity-theory.html.

[16] Storey, Sylvana. "Unconscious Bias -- Making Millions From Theory." The Huffington Post. January 15, 2017. Accessed May 03, 2018. https://www.huffingtonpost.com/sylvana-storey/unconscious-bias-making-m_b_8771258.html.

[17] Ross, Howard J. *Everyday Bias: Identifying and Navigating Unconscious Judgments in Our Daily Lives.* Place of Publication Not Identified: Rowman & Littlefield, 2016.

[18] "Philtrum." Dictionary.com. Accessed May 03, 2018. http://www.dictionary.com/browse/philtrum.

[19] "Neuroplasticity." Dictionary.com. Accessed May 03, 2018. http://www.dictionary.com/browse/neuroplasticity.

[20] Hampton, Debbie. "Neuroplasticity: The 10 Fundamentals Of Rewiring Your Brain." Reset.me. October 28, 2015. Accessed May 03, 2018. http://reset.me/story/neuroplasticity-the-10-fundamentals-of-rewiring-your-brain/.

[21] "Project Implicit." Select a Test. Accessed May 10, 2018. https://implicit.harvard.edu/implicit/.

[22] *Ibid.*

[23] "Privilege." Dictionary.com. Accessed May 03, 2018. http://www.dictionary.com/browse/privilege.

[24] Hill, Catey. "6 times It's More Expensive to Be a Woman." MarketWatch. April 12, 2016. Accessed May 03, 2018. https://www.marketwatch.com/story/5-things-women-pay-more-for-than-men-2014-01-17.

[25] "Groupthink." Dictionary.com. Accessed May 03, 2018. http://www.dictionary.com/browse/groupthink.

[26] "Self-image." Dictionary.com. Accessed May 03, 2018. http://www.dictionary.com/browse/self-image.

[27] Rath, Tom. *Strengthsfinder 2.0.* New York: Gallup Press, 2017.

[28] Rath, Tom, and Barry Conchie. *Strengths Based Leadership.* 1st ed. Gallup Press, 2008.

[29] "CliftonStrengths | Gallup." Sign In | Gallup. Accessed May 10, 2018. https://www.gallupstrengthscenter.com/home/en-us.

[30] "How to Fascinate." Personality Test. Accessed May 10, 2018. https://www.howtofascinate.com/.

[31] Hogshead, Sally. *How the World Sees You: Discover Your Highest Value through the Science of Fascination.* New York, NY: Harper Business, an Imprint of HarperCollinsPublishers, 2014.

[32] Hogshead, Sally. *Fascinate: Your 7 Triggers to Persuasion and Captivation.* New York: Harper Business, 2010.

[33] "DiSC Profile - What Is DiSC®? The DiSC Personality Profile Explained." DiSCProfile.com. Accessed May 10, 2018. https://www.discprofile.com/what-is-disc/overview/.

[34] The Myers & Briggs Foundation - MBTI® Basics. Accessed May 10, 2018. http://www.myersbriggs.org/my-mbti-personality-type/mbti-basics/home.htm?bhcp=1.

[35] "The Sorting Hat." Pottermore. Accessed May 10, 2018. https://www.pottermore.com/writing-by-jk-rowling/the-sorting-hat.

[36] Robinson, Melia. "Tim Ferriss: 'You Are the Average of the Five People You Most Associate With'." *Business Insider*. January 11, 2017. Accessed May 03, 2018. http://www.businessinsider.com/tim-ferriss-average-of-five-people-2017-1.

[37] "Customer." Merriam-Webster. Accessed May 03, 2018. https://www.merriam-webster.com/dictionary/customer.

[38] "Mentor." Merriam-Webster. Accessed May 03, 2018. https://www.merriam-webster.com/dictionary/mentor.

[39] Murphy, Mark. "The Dunning-Kruger Effect Shows Why Some People Think They're Great Even When Their Work Is Terrible." Forbes. January 24, 2017. Accessed May 08, 2018. https://www.forbes.com/sites/markmurphy/2017/01/24/the-dunning-kruger-effect-shows-why-some-people-think-theyre-great-even-when-their-work-is-terrible/#3daa9fc5d7c9.

[40] Clance, Pauline Rose, and Suzanne Ament Imes. "The Imposter Phenomenon in High Achieving Women: Dynamics and Therapeutic Intervention." *Psychotherapy: Theory, Research & Practice* 15, no. 3 (1978): 241-47. Accessed May 3, 2018. doi:10.1037/h0086006.

[41] Corkindale, Gill. "Overcoming Imposter Syndrome." Harvard Business Review. May/June, 2008. Accessed May 03, 2018. https://hbr.org/2008/05/overcoming-imposter-syndrome.

[42] Task, Aaron. "Dick Parsons Explains What Crisis Management Is All About." Fortune. August 22, 2016. Accessed May 03, 2018. http://fortune.com/2016/08/22/dick-parsons-fortune-unfiltered/.

[43] Nye, Bill. "Commencement Address." Address, Lowell, MA, 2014.

[44] Lohmann, Rachel Cassada, MS, LPCS. "Achieving Happiness by Helping Others." Psychology Today. January 29, 2017. Accessed May 03, 2018. https://www.psychologytoday.com/us/blog/teen-angst/201701/achieving-happiness-helping-others.

[45] Gale, Porter. *Your Network Is Your Net Worth: Unlock the Hidden Power of Connections for Wealth, Success, and Happiness in the Digital Age.* New York: Atria Books, 2013.

[46] "Network." Dictionary.com. Accessed May 03, 2018. http://www.dictionary.com/browse/network.

[47] Sims, David. "Seinfeld: "The Bizarro Jerry"/"The Little Kicks"." TV Club. November 10, 2011. Accessed May 03, 2018. https://tv.avclub.com/seinfeld-the-bizarro-jerry-the-little-kicks-1798170418.

[48] Deutschendorf, Harvey. "5 Reasons You Should Hang Out With People Who Are Different From You." *Fast Company.* August 21, 2014. Accessed May 03, 2018. https://www.fastcompany.com/3034602/5-reasons-to-hang-out-with-people-that-are-different-from-us.

[49] Institute for Diversity Certification (IDC), The. *CDP Exam Study Guide.* 4th ed. 2016. Page 27.

[50] Fry, Richard. "Millennials Are the Largest Generation in the U.S. Labor Force." Pew Research Center. April 11, 2018. Accessed May 10, 2018. http://www.pewresearch.org/fact-tank/2018/04/11/millennials-largest-generation-us-labor-force/.

[51] *Ibid.*

[52] Age Discrimination in Employment Act of 1967 (ADEA) (1967).

[53] 29 U.S. Code, § 14-631.

[54] Gosselin, Peter, and Ariana Tobin. "Cutting 'Old Heads' at IBM." ProPublica. March 22, 2018. Accessed May 03, 2018. https://features.propublica.org/ibm/ibm-age-discrimination-american-workers/.

[55] Zetlin, Minda. "12 Ways Women Unknowingly Sabotage Their Success." *Business Insider.* February 11, 2015. Accessed May 03, 2018. http://www.businessinsider.com/ways-women-sabotage-their-success-2015-2.

[56] Mohr, Tara Sophia. "Why Women Don't Apply for Jobs Unless They're 100% Qualified." HBR.org. August 25, 2014. Accessed May 29, 2018. https://hbr.org/2014/08/why-women-dont-apply-for-jobs-unless-theyre-100-qualified

[57] "Uptalk | Definition of Uptalk in English by Oxford Dictionaries." Oxford Dictionaries | English. Accessed May 03, 2018. https://en.oxforddictionaries.com/definition/uptalk.

[58] Linneman, Thomas. "Linneman: Use of 'uptalk' on Jeopardy." YouTube. March 14, 2014. Accessed May 03, 2018. https://www.youtube.com/watch?v=4dRa_qPBguE.

[59] Gross, Jessica. "What Can Jeopardy Tell Us About Uptalk?" Smithsonian.com. January 01, 2014. Accessed May 03, 2018. http://www.smithsonianmag.com/innovation/what-can-jeopardy-tell-us-about-uptalk-180948000/?no-ist.

[60] Boylan, Jennifer Finney. *Shes Not There: A Life in Two Genders.* New York: Broadway Paperbacks, 2013.

[61] Flores, Andrew R., Jody L. Herman, Gary J. Gates, and Taylor N. T. Brown. *How Many Adults Identify as Transgender in the United States?*UCLA School of Law. The Williams Institute. June 2016. https://williamsinstitute.law.ucla.edu/wp-content/uploads/How-Many-Adults-Identify-as-Transgender-in-the-United-States.pdf.

[62] Kertscher, Tom. "How Many People in the Military Are Transgender?" PolitiFact Wisconsin. July 26, 2017. Accessed May 03, 2018. http://www.politifact.com/wisconsin/statements/2017/jul/26/mark-pocan/how-many-people-military-are-transgender/.

[63] Human Rights Campaign. "State Maps of Laws & Policies: Employment." HRC.org. April 25, 2017. Accessed May 3, 2018. https://www.hrc.org/state-maps/employment.

[64] Human Rights Campaign. "State Maps of Laws & Policies: Housing." HRC.org. April 25, 2017. Accessed May 3, 2018. Human Rights Campaign. "State Maps of Laws & Policies." HRC.org. April 25, 2017. Accessed May 3, 2018. https://www.hrc.org/state-maps/housing.

[65] Center for American Progress, and Movement Advancement Project. *Paying an Unfair Price: The Financial Penalty for Being Transgender in America.* LGBTMap.org. February 2015. Accessed May 3, 2018. http://www.lgbtmap.org/file/paying-an-unfair-price-transgender.pdf.

[66] Human Rights Campaign. "State Maps of Laws & Policies: Hate Crimes." HRC.org. December 01, 2017. https://www.hrc.org/state-maps/hate-crimes.

[67] Human Rights Campaign. "Violence Against the Transgender Community in 2017." Human Rights Campaign. Accessed May 03, 2018. https://www.hrc.org/resources/violence-against-the-transgender-community-in-2017.

[68] Human Rights Campaign. "Sexual Assault and the LGBTQ Community." Human Rights Campaign. Accessed May 09, 2018. https://www.hrc.org/resources/sexual-assault-and-the-lgbt-community.

[69] Seigler, Carrie. "Combating LGBT Street Harassment One Conversation at a Time." GLAAD. June 24, 2015. Accessed May 09, 2018. https://www.glaad.org/blog/combating-lgbt-street-harassment-one-conversation-time.

[70] Rodriguez-Roldan, Victoria. "The Criminal Justice System Is Broken and Trans People Are Suffering." Advocate.com. May 24, 2016. Accessed May 09, 2018. https://www.advocate.com/commentary/2016/5/24/criminal-justice-system-broken-and-trans-people-are-suffering.

[71] Haas, Ann P., Ph.D., Philip L. Rodgers, Ph.D., and Jody L. Herman, Ph.D. *Suicide Attempts among Transgender and Gender Non-Conforming Adults: Findings of the National Transgender Discrimination Survey.* UCLA School of Law. The Williams Institute. January 2014. Accessed May 3, 2018. Human Rights Campaign. "Violence Against the Transgender Community in 2017." Human Rights Campaign. Accessed May 03, 2018. https://www.hrc.org/resources/violence-against-the-transgender-community-in-2017.

[72] Mendelsohn, Michaela. "Executive Leadership Panel." Speech, 20th Annual ROMBA Conference, Boston Seaport World Trade Center, Boston, MA, October 14, 2017.

[73] "GLAAD Media Reference Guide – Transgender." GLAAD. Accessed May 26, 2018. https://www.glaad.org/reference/transgender.

[74] *Ibid.*

[75] "ERGs (Employee Resource Groups)." Catalyst. Accessed May 03, 2018. http://www.catalyst.org/knowledge/topics/ergs-employee-resource-groups.

[76] Park, Jung. "3 Challenges for Asian Americans in The Workplace." The Typical Asian: The Blog for Asian America. March 24, 2016. Accessed May 03, 2018. https://blogs.baruch.cuny.edu/thetypicalasian/top-lists/3-challenges-for-asian-americans-in-the-workplace/.

[77] Arizona Republic, The. "ASU Study: Men More Likely to Think They're Smart; Women Downplay Intelligence." Arizona State University. April 09, 2018. Accessed May 03, 2018. https://research.asu.edu/news-events/asu-study-men-more-likely-think-theyre-smart-women-downplay-intelligence.

[78] Corporate Leadership Council. (2004). *Driving Performance and Retention Through Employee Engagement*[Scholarly project]. In *Corporate Leadership Council*. Retrieved May 15, 2018, from www.corporateleadershipcouncil.com

[79] Beattie, Geoffrey, and Patrick Johnson. "Possible Unconscious Bias in Recruitment and Promotion and the Need to Promote Equality." *Perspectives: Policy and Practice in Higher Education*16, no. 1 (2012): 7-13. doi:10.1080/13603108.2011.611833.

[80] "Inclusive Leadership Conference - Déclic International." Declic International. July 05, 2017. Accessed May 03, 2018. http://declicinternational.com.

[81] Bishop, Elli. "6 Brands That Succeed At Understanding Hispanic Marketing." Business 2 Community. October 7, 2014. Accessed May 03, 2018. https://www.business2community.com/marketing/6-brands-succeed-understanding-hispanic-marketing-01030311#b36hfZguFXpjxMHi.97.

[82] Brown, Jennifer, and Jude DiClemente. "Harnessing the Power of LGBT Employee Resource Groups (ERGs)." The Glasshammer. March 12, 2015. Accessed May 03, 2018. http://theglasshammer.com/2011/06/21/harnessing-the-power-of-lgbt-employee-resource-groups-ergs/.

[83] "Latinx | Definition of Latinx in English by Oxford Dictionaries." Oxford Dictionaries | English. Accessed May 03, 2018. https://en.oxforddictionaries.com/definition/latinx.

[84] "Stereotype | Definition of Stereotype in English by Oxford Dictionaries." Oxford Dictionaries | English. Accessed May 03, 2018. https://en.oxforddictionaries.com/definition/stereotype.

[85] "Ally | Definition of Ally in English by Oxford Dictionaries." Oxford Dictionaries | English. Accessed May 03, 2018. https://en.oxforddictionaries.com/definition/ally.

[86] National Alliance on Mental Illness. "Mental Health by the Numbers." NAMI.org. Accessed May 03, 2018. https://www.nami.org/learn-more/mental-health-by-the-numbers.

[87] United States Census Bureau. "Nearly 1 in 5 People Have a Disability in the U.S., Census Bureau Reports." Newsroom Archive. May 19, 2016. Accessed May 03, 2018. https://www.census.gov/newsroom/releases/archives/miscellaneous/cb12-134.html.

[88] Carroll, Joseph. "U.S. Crime Victimization Trends Flat." Gallup.com. November 09, 2007. Accessed May 03, 2018. http://news.gallup.com/poll/102658/us-crime-victimization-trends-flat.aspx.

[89] Link, Bruce G., Ph.D., Ezra Susser, M.D., Ann Stueve, Ph.D., Jo Phelan, Ph.D., Robert E. Moore, Dr.Ph., and Elmer Struening, Ph.D. "Lifetime and Five-year Prevalence of Homelessness in the United States." *American Journal of Public Health* 84, no. 12 (December 1994): 1907-912. Accessed May 3, 2018. doi:10.2105/ajph.84.12.1907.

[90] United States. Department of Justice. Office of Justice Programs. *Lifetime Likelihood of Going to State or Federal Prison*. By Thomas P. Bonczar and Allen J. Beck, Ph.D. 1997. March 1997. Accessed May 3, 2018. https://bjs.gov/content/pub/pdf/Llgsfp.pdf.

[91] Feliz, Josie. "Survey: Ten Percent of American Adults Report Being in Recovery from Substance Abuse or Addiction." Partnership for Drug-Free Kids - Where Families Find Answers. March 06, 2012. Accessed May 03, 2018. https://drugfree.org/newsroom/news-item/survey-ten-percent-of-american-adults-report-being-in-recovery-from-substance-abuse-or-addiction/.

[92] "Statistics." National Cancer Institute. Accessed May 03, 2018. https://cancercontrol.cancer.gov/ocs/statistics/statistics.html.

[93] Human Rights Campaign. (n.d.). HRC Study Shows Majority of LGBT Workers Closeted at the Workplace. Retrieved May 15, 2018, from https://www.hrc.org/blog/hrc-study-shows-majority-of-lgbt-workers-closeted-on-the-job

[94] 2017 Workplace Equality Fact Sheet. (2017, December 13). Retrieved May 15, 2018, from http://outandequal.org/2017-workplace-equality-fact-sheet/

[95] Goffman, E. (1990). *Stigma: Notes on the management of spoiled identity*. London: Penguin Books.

[96] Yoshino, Kenji. (2007). *Covering: The hidden assault on our civil rights*. New York: Random House.

[97] "Microaggression." Merriam-Webster. Accessed May 03, 2018. https://www.merriam-webster.com/dictionary/microaggression.

[98] Newstrom, John W., and Keith Davis. Organizational Behavior: Human Behavior at Work. Page 103. New York: McGraw-Hill, 1993.

[99] "Transparent." Merriam-Webster. Accessed May 03, 2018. https://www.merriam-webster.com/dictionary/transparent.

[100] "Authentic." Merriam-Webster. Accessed May 03, 2018. https://www.merriam-webster.com/dictionary/authentic.

[101] "Vulnerable." Merriam-Webster. Accessed May 03, 2018. https://www.merriam-webster.com/dictionary/vulnerable.

[102] "Accept." Merriam-Webster. Accessed May 03, 2018. https://www.merriam-webster.com/dictionary/accept.

[103] Covey, Stephen R. *The 7 Habits of Highly Effective People: Powerful Lessons in Personal Change*. New York: Fireside Press, 1989.

[104] Bradberry, Travis, and Jean Greaves. *Emotional Intelligence 2.0*. San Diego, CA: TalentSmart, 2009.

[105] Catalyst. "Women CEOs of the S&P 500." Catalyst. May 03, 2018. Accessed May 03, 2018. http://www.catalyst.org/knowledge/women-ceos-sp-500.

[106] United States Department of Labor. "Women in the Labor Force in 2010." United States Department of Labor. Accessed May 03, 2018. https://www.dol.gov/wb/factsheets/qf-laborforce-10.htm.

[107] Bidwell, Allie. "Women More Likely to Graduate College, but Still Earn Less Than Men." *U.S. News & World Report*. October 31, 2014. Accessed May 03, 2018. https://www.usnews.com/news/blogs/data-mine/2014/10/31/women-more-likely-to-graduate-college-but-still-earn-less-than-men.

[108] "Black Fortune 500 CEO's: Black Entrepreneurs, Black CEO, Black Executive, Black Billionaires, Entrepreneur Profile." Black Entrepreneur & Executive Profiles. Accessed May 03, 2018. https://www.blackentrepreneurprofile.com/fortune-500-ceos/.

[109] *Ibid.*

[110] *Ibid.*

Made in the USA
Lexington, KY
02 October 2018